HAUNTED
STAFFORDSHIRE

HAUNTED
STAFFORDSHIRE

Philip Solomon

The
History
Press

This book is dedicated to my grandchildren, Liam and Elise, who both mean the world to me. A special acknowledgement is also due to my wife, Kath, who helped with my research, typing up of the manuscript, photography and so much more. Without her help, this book would not have been possible.

First published 2012

The History Press
The Mill, Brimscombe Port
Stroud, Gloucestershire, GL5 2QG
www.thehistorypress.co.uk

British Library Cataloguing in Publication Data.
A catalogue record for this book is available from the British Library.

ISBN 978 0 7524 6168 7
Typesetting and origination by The History Press
Printed in Great Britain
Manufacturing managed by Jellyfish Print Solutions Ltd

Contents

Acknowledgements

All libraries and all contributors, too numerous to mention, who provided stories for this book, I acknowledge and thank you all.

I would also like to thank the following:

Lesley Smith and the team at Tutbury Castle for pictures of Tutbury Castle
Martyn Boyes and Haunted Happenings for pictures of Tutbury Castle
Liz West and Alton Towers for pictures of Alton Towers
Jo Pritchard for the picture of Tamworth Castle
Jenny Brown for her pictures of Middleton Hall
Karen Westwood and Team Prism for the picture of Drakelow Tunnels

Thanks also to Graham Parnell Walsh for his drawings and artistic impressions.

Introduction

LET'S start with a question – what is a ghost? The answer is that we don't really know what it is. The word is one we use to describe something that we cannot explain. Electricity is not, for example, a *tangible* thing like a building. We can describe what a building is, but all we can really say about electricity is that it is energy. The same, I suppose, applies to ghosts. We know something about the way they behave, but we can't really explain this phenomena, just as we can't explain of how electrons move around the way they do to make electricity; they just do.

In my experience, an upset or crisis can lead to unusual mental effects. For every case of an apparition, there are hundreds of others that involve telepathy. So let's consider telepathy – a phrase actually coined in 1882 by the Society of Psychical Research to describe the transfer of information from one place to another without the use of any of the known senses. Today we know a good deal about the way in which telepathy works, and we have even found ways of demonstrating it in the laboratory under controlled conditions.

A feature of telepathy is that it operates regardless of distance. It seems reasonable, therefore, to suppose that since space does not inhibit its effects, neither does time. If this is so, then some haunting symptoms would become a little easier to understand.

Some hauntings suggest that when people are in a state of great crisis, a kind of 'tape-recording' may be made of their respective states. Those sensitive to ethereal auras, such as psychics, clairvoyants, and clairaudients, can see or play back that 'tape' and see it repeated again and again, and thus an apparition forms.

Unfortunately, I have to say that at the present time we have no understanding of *how* this recording or play-back mechanism comes about. We can, however, assume that a ghost is a phenomenon that may result perhaps from two causes: a) a living person or b) a memory record. We may not always need both causes and one may indeed create the other. We also know that some psychic phenomena can be created to order with a little practice. I have sat at séances myself and also with other

A Ouija board – a tool occasionally used during a séance.

psychics that leave me in no doubt that this is possible.

Let us now go through the various types of haunting. We can see, or rather I hope you will see, that some of them are easier to ascribe to one cause or the other. However, I shall now try to summarise for you the top five reasons behind a haunting.

1 – Apparitions

Examples of apparitions have been reported in 50 per cent of the cases that I have personally investigated. Some apparitions have appeared so genuinely lifelike that those who see them have believed they were living people. Others have been the more transparent, typically ghost-like apparitions. However, in the case of lifelike spectres, the identity of a ghost is often inferred at the accord of the witness; thereby it cannot be ruled out that the human mind could indeed be playing mischievous tricks. We should always be aware of that fact when investigating ghosts and the paranormal in the wider context.

Generally speaking, our eyes serve us extremely well and send true visions back to the brain. However, there are times when one's visual perception of things is not always what it seems. Many psychologists, for instance, have turned to illusions in which perceptions of things are confusing and misleading to get a better knowledge and understanding of that process. Scientists, for many years, have studied geometrical illusions, and, despite various individuals hypothesising explanations, no one has ever really reached a situation where they know exactly how they work. I do think it is important when considering ghosts and hauntings, in the wider context, to be aware of these 'tricks of the eyes'. However, all this aside, when similar apparitions are seen independently by different witnesses, the 'all in the mind' or 'trick of the eyes' theories begin to look rather weak.

2 – Unexplained Footsteps

There have been numerous cases of people reporting the sound of footsteps – far too many cases, in my opinion, for us to ascribe all of them to misunderstanding, misinterpretation of sound and so on, and a lot of them have led me to conduct an immediate investigation. Footsteps are often heard by the most down-to-earth people; policemen, firemen, teachers, school caretakers, librarians, and so on. In fact, this is the one most objective of the various types of hauntings and of course is one of the strongest cases for the memory record there is.

3 – The Movement of Objects

The unexplained movement of objects, large and small, has been reported time and time again in some form or another in around 25 per cent of the cases I have investigated. Doors that open and shut on their own are common, as are vases that fly across rooms, and electronic equipment that switches itself on and off. Now the opening and closing of doors can sometimes have an explanation – subsidence in the building, badly fitting frames causing the door to open on its own, and so on. The switching on and off of electronic equipment, such as a television or a radio, however, can be a little more difficult to explain.

4 – Cold Spots

This seems to be a wholly objective phenomena and it is one I have witnessed myself time and time again. With the rapidly-increasing availability of video recording equipment and facilities for

A Halloween event at the Black Country Living Museum.

infrared heat-sensitive photography, there is a reasonable chance that one of these days one of these cold spots may produce a ghost for us on film. Time and time again, ghostly happenings and hauntings have happened around areas known as cold spots.

5 – Dates or Times of the Year

A question I am often asked is whether there are special times of the year when ghosts can be seen. I am not entirely convinced that there are special times when ghosts appear, but many experts insist there are certain nights of the year when a special magic exists, if you will, which allows spirits or ghosts to return to the earth plane in greater numbers.

The most famous of all dates is probably 31 October – All Hallows' Eve, or Halloween as we call it today. The origins of Halloween lie in a pagan festival of fire and death, which highlighted the powers of darkness. It marked the beginning of winter and the passing away of the old year. It is said that this is the time when the dead abound in search of other lost souls and in Staffordshire, especially in the country areas, offerings of food and drink were left for them as they passed westwards towards the direction of the 'death' of the sun and sunset.

In the seventh century, All Hallows' Eve became the eve of All Saints Day, which was a feast day to celebrate the various saints and martyrs and was most probably done to make the pagan festival of the dead more akin with Christianity.

All Souls' Day is a celebration in the Roman Catholic faith and is held on 2 November, when prayers are offered for the souls of all of those who have passed to the higher life. Perhaps these prayers have something to do with the many reports year after year of ghostly apparitions around this time and maybe they do help, for it is a fact that more ghosts are reported around Halloween than any other time of the year.

The only other day that is reputed to be anywhere near as magical or haunted as Halloween is Christmas Eve, when many ghostly appearances are reported, some very famous ones at that, including the ghost of Queen Anne Boleyn walking the bridge that spans the River Eden at Hever Castle in Kent, and the ghost of Charles Dickens in the burial grounds of Rochester Castle, also in Kent. In recent years I have been told of a headless horseman who annually appears in various parts of Staffordshire and of the ghost of an old hag that appears in and around Cannock.

However, 20 June, mid-Summer's eve, is also historically reported to be a good time to see ghosts and it is claimed that many people, especially in Staffordshire and certain parts of the Black Country, apparently used to cast various charms to attract spirits and fairies in years gone by. The 12th of February is the anniversary date of the execution of Lady Jane Grey, and there have been reports of cries and moans being heard in Enville village, which is quite close to Kinver. Perhaps the ghostly sounds are made by members of her family, who are known to have lived at Enville Hall before and after the death of the 'nine day Queen'.

The 5th of November, Bonfire Night, or Guy Fawkes Night, is also alleged to

The author looking for ghostly fingerprints.

be a great night for ghost spotting. These bonfires were originally lit for pagan reasons and had nothing at all to do with Bonfire Night as we know it today. Perhaps the many lights all over the country that reach up to the sky are what really attract ghosts and spirits. Originally, these bonfires provided light and heat through the dark winter months in Celtic countries.

If you are interested in looking for ghosts at the so-called 'special' times of the year, it might be worthwhile to look at the numerous historical dates and anniversaries that seem to cause the appearance of ghosts on a particularly significant day. But you have to remember that ghosts do not appear on demand and the worst possible thing to do if you really want to see a ghost is to *try* to see one, for it is highly likely that you won't! There is a logical explanation for this, as many psychic experiences occur when

people are in a relaxed or calm state, sometimes just before they drop off to sleep or just before they wake up, or even perhaps while daydreaming. Often, hauntings occur when people are going about their everyday, routine jobs or chores.

When we are considering supernatural phenomena, we should remember that we have two quite different modes of consciousness, and which one we are in depends on which side of our brain is dominant. If the left side is in charge, we reject any information we cannot explain. If we come across something improbable in this state, such as a ghost, we persuade ourselves that there must be a normal explanation even when that is less probable than the actual phenomenon itself!

When the right side gets a chance to take over, most likely when we are in a relaxed state, then what happens can be very interesting. For many people, the quickest way to relax the left side of the mind is to drink a small amount of alcohol. In this way, we are far more open to new impressions and probably in one of the best possible states of mind in which to experience a ghostly encounter.

A lot of investigators of the paranormal, such as parapsychologists and ghost hunters, have given me quite a lot of stick for suggesting that some of the best evidence for the existence of ghosts has been found by amateurs with a very simple kit; this can be made up from everyday items around the home, such as a tape recorder, a camera with a built-in flash, adhesive tape, a good thermometer and spare batteries. Of course, there is some very technical equipment on the market, such as electromagnetic field meters, electronic thermometers, night-scopes, light intensifying binoculars, thermal imaging cameras and many other things that have become available to purchase in more recent years. Personally, I just don't think they are worth the money, and they certainly don't guarantee that you will have a paranormal experience.

The worst possible attitude towards ghosts and hauntings, in my experience, is to be in a state of fear – which is strange really, because most people love to be scared. But we enjoy watching horror films, for example, because we know it is safe. We know that Boris Karloff or Dracula will not step out of our television sets and shake us by the scruff of our necks – we are in the position to switch it off and exercise complete control over the situation. We may be scared during the film but that fright is only temporary and it is explainable.

However, we are now considering frightening things which happen in real life, although a lot of us refuse to accept that it is possible even if they have happened to us, for it creates a kind of mental conflict within us. Aside from very rare cases, there is no real reason to be frightened of anything a ghost might do. Are you really scared by the sight of an old hooded monk or a Grey Lady or even the Highwayman of Kinver and Whittington. Are you really scared of them just because they are dead, or because they represent the unknown? Confront your fears! Read on and learn of the many ghosts, hauntings and legends of Staffordshire…

Philip Solomon, 2012

1
A Brief History of Haunted Staffordshire

HISTORICALLY speaking, Staffordshire included Wolverhampton, Walsall and West Bromwich, which were taken away from Staffordshire in 1974 to be placed in the new county of the West Midlands, leaving the administrative area of Staffordshire as a narrow southward protrusion that runs west to the border of Worcestershire, further on to the city of Stoke-on-Trent. In the 1990s, however, Stoke-on-Trent was removed to form a unitary authority, but still remains, and is considered by most, as part of Staffordshire. In its ancient history, it was broken down into the five areas of Seisdon, Totmonslow, Cuttlestone, Offlow and Pirehill.

It is believed 913 was the year when Stafford, became a fortified military stronghold for the capital of Mercia under the rule of Queen Aethelflaed. The county is symbolised by the famous Stafford Knot (often mistakenly called the Staffordshire Knat), which can be seen on an Anglican stone cross that dates from approximately 805. The cross still stands proud in Stoke churchyard, so the symbol of the knot may be considered either an ancient Mercian symbol or one that was adopted from ancient Celtic and Christian traditions, which had been brought to Stafford by Lindisfarne monks in the year 650.

Staffordshire is many things to many people; from the area's close links to the industrialised Black Country in the south of the county, to the more craggy regions to the north and its moorlands, which have beautiful country regions; each place still manages to retain a sense of individual pride. One famous son and writer of Staffordshire was Arnold Bennett, who came up with the phrase 'the five towns for the potteries' and describes the county very well in his book, *The Old Wives' Tale*. To the south of the county lies the famous Cannock Chase, where, historically, kings and princes hunted, and there are numerous ghost stories and legends told within the pages of that book of this most beautiful place.

Much of Staffordshire to the south of the Trent was originally part of the huge forest making up the royal forests of Cannock and Kinver, together with the

Needswood Forest, where the legends of Robin Hood, and his 'merry men', made their mark. Most of the forest and its trees have been cut down over the years, a great deal of it in the Middle Ages, to smelt ironstone.

The Romans also played their part in Staffordshire history and helped to create legends and wonderful romantic stories, including haunted ones too. But before them, Staffordshire was lived in and revered by people who prayed to the earth and the great goddess Earth Mother. To the north of the area, Brigit still has legends that retain stories of her reign at the Bridestones, whereas Woden is mentioned in the name Wednesbury.

Staffordshire was believed to be home to the Celtic Priest Order, the Druids, and also the Ovates. Throughout the county there are still sites that have stones and waters that are said to heal and balance, and the myths and legends are still there to be found with a little research. So, join me as I take you on a tour of one of England's oldest shires and introduce you to its spooks and spectres.

2
Ghost Stories

Royal Oak Inn, Abbots Bromley

It is here that a tall gentleman with a full beard was seen some years ago by several people in the attic area and also in one of the bathrooms. No one really knows for sure who this figure could be, but some people refer to him as 'Laughing Charlie'. Other people have heard the sound of a music box playing when no item of that sort was located nearby. No one knows for sure what the tune was, but some think it may have been The Merry Widow. Although the music was heard in the bar area, it seemed to be coming from far away, perhaps from another world!

Acton Trussell

The Moat House Hotel in Acton Trussell, not far from Stafford, is a nice place to spend time walking around the grounds. It also has a good restaurant and a romantic ambience, hence the reason why many people choose it as a venue for their wedding reception.

Part of the building was built in the fifteenth century, and, over time, there have been a lot of alterations to the medieval moat manor house. Unsurprisingly, then, it is no wonder that people have reported the sounds of laughter and conversations from yesteryear when no one is to be seen.

Perhaps the most famous resident ghost is a gentleman the staff simply refer to as George. Rumour has it that if alterations to the building were to take place, it was best to announce the work aloud before commencing it so that George was aware of the changes; otherwise it was not unusual for building work to go wrong and for tools to move round of their own accord. The staff also said that George puts in the occasional appearance dressed in fifteenth-century clothes in the part of the building that dates back to that century, and, although he is not seen anywhere near as regularly as in the past, when he does appear for someone, it is usually an indication that some changes to the building are about to occur. Perhaps he has an ability of foresight from the other side – who can say?

The Lea House, Adbaston

Here we come across a story from the 1800s of Madam Vernon, who is said to have returned to her home shortly after her death, angry at the way the family had divided her lands and money. There were reports that her spirit communicated these feelings by causing a great deal of problems around the building, throwing things around and generally scared people witless. This poltergeist activity reached such a frequency that eventually a local clergyman gained permission to conduct an exorcism to banish the entity. It was claimed that a pond lay directly underneath the house, and this was where the spectre was sent – to some degree, this seems to have since quietened the haunting. However, other people continue to speak of witnessing Madam Vernon's anger, with some even claiming to have seen the spectre shaking her finger in temper.

Alton Towers

The theme park has been the site of many reported ghost sightings and is a place I have visited on numerous occasions as part of paranormal investigation teams. People describe seeing the vision of a gypsy lady that roams the building. Perhaps one of the most interesting stories is that of The Chained Oak. During the eighteenth century, the Earl of Shrewsbury invited many of the aristocracy and nobles of Europe to a fabulous banquet at the newly improved Alton Towers. All forms of entertainers and musicians were brought to the site to entertain those present.

Everyone was having a fabulous time until, suddenly, the music came to a halt and everyone's attention was drawn to an elderly man with long hair and in a very poor state of dress. No one knew how he had managed to get into the grounds or attend the banquet, for he would have surely been stopped by servants with the responsibility of keeping out those considered to be of a lower order. The earl was furious and insisted the old man explain his presence. The man said that he was a Romany fortune-telling traveller and hoped the earl would provide him with a little food and sustenance in exchange for telling the fortune of some of his guests.

The earl would have none of it, and ordered his men to drag him from the estate. The guests, wishing to please their revered host, jeered and laughed at the old man but fell silent as he shouted back at the earl and gave a terrible warning; every time a branch fell from the oak tree in his grounds, one of his family would die. Still the earl laughed and the party resumed with great vigour. But something had rung fear in the mind of the earl, for the very next day, after his guests had left, he ordered the head gardener and his team to fasten strong chains around all the heavier branches of the oak so that none could fall.

Those who visit Alton Towers will note that the chains are still there to this day. The Hex ride is very close to the ancient oak and one of the Tower's most popular rides. As people queue to take their turn on the Hex, some have spoken of seeing a figure in black, others of a ghost dressed in riding apparel. I am not surprised by this as I have

Alton Towers.

seen for myself such a figure and also a black horse, which has also been reported.

One of the most reported ghosts, however, is that of the Black Lady. Also commonly reported is the smell of roses and lavender. Many people believe, with great authority, that the ghosts still pacing around the towers are from the Talbot family – particularly Charles, who had been forced to sell the property due to financial difficulties. Also sighted are a man described as a hunchback, a black dog, and voices that seem to echo in a most sinister way, not just in the hours of darkness, but during the daylight too.

Strangely enough, the ladies' toilets seem to attract a lot of paranormal activity. Mrs Buckle, who worked at the site for many years, seemed to be particularly sensitive to such shades, and was even brave enough to address what she called a ghost in a black cloak, tall hat and boots. Mrs Buckle felt that the character she witnessed was perhaps not happy with the changes and alterations to the park over the years.

There is another story of a young lady who wished to make a marriage that was considered to be below her status and that her father had her locked in a high tower, where she either fell or threw herself to her death. Some people believe that on that particular night, a horse had been saddled and was waiting for her – this may be the same answer ghost that is seen in riding gear, possibly a prospective bridegroom.

Barton-under-Needwood

At one time this area was the home of the Royal Airforce base at Tatenhill. In more recent years the site has been used as a large warehouse. Several people have reported smelling a fragrance rather like an old-fashioned aftershave or cologne that always seems to waft around one particular corner of the warehouse, strangely at very specific times – often around 8.30 p.m. in the evening. Other witnesses describe the smell of a Woodbine cigarette, popular during the First World War and up to the 1960s. Perhaps even more surprising was finding what was described as a nub-end of a cigarette, plain and without a tip, when no one who entered that building smoked such a cigarette. Other people have reported the sound of young men's voices in the building, shouting and laughing with one another when it was definitely empty. This is a modern ghost story that can be placed around 2008, and a most interesting one at that.

Bucknell

I have worked on many paranormal investigations, and one thing I always tell people is that it is vitally important to look for a rational explanation before shouting 'ghost'. I think an excellent example of this can be found in Marian Pipe's super book, *Secret Staffordshire, Ghosts, Legends and Strange Tales*, in which she presents the story of the demon donkey. In Hanley, there was a most interesting individual known by the name of Sauntering Ned, who made his living selling pottery that he carried in the leather panniers strapped to the sides of his faithful donkey. Making a living was hard in the 1790s, and Ned feared robbery in some of the more secluded lanes and tracks of Staffordshire, which could be pitch black and scary at the best of times. So he fashioned a mask complete with horns that his donkey could wear and held a small candle between them so as to present a most demonic-looking sight for anyone who came upon them with sinister intentions. One night, as man and beast were making their way back to Hanley, he found himself passing Bucknall Church, a place he felt robbers might be lying in wait. Stopping for a moment to light the candle, he noticed the light from another candle in the churchyard itself and thought he could hear the sound of digging. His curiosity getting the better of him, he led his donkey towards the light and came upon an open grave. Inside stood two men, spades in hand, who were about to open a coffin. As they looked up, one man screamed, 'It's the Devil himself come for us!' With great haste, the two men fled the scene, leaving their tools, a good horse, and a quite use-able cart behind them. Ned decided to take their property, and, as the men were never heard of again, was able to make considerable use of them in his business thenceforth. So you see, an answer can often be found without resorting to a paranormal explanation. What a good job Ned and his faithful donkey performed that night!

Blithfield Hall

This hall was once home to the Bagot family. Many ghosts allegedly haunt the site. One spectre sometimes appears in the lower gallery, and sometimes you can hear the sound of clothes dragging on the floor, which would suggest a female spirit wearing a long dress, but some people associated with the building feel it is more likely to be the energy of a monk who may have been concealed at the hall to avoid capture at a time when many were persecuted for their religion.

Blithfield is also the regular haunting ground of the Grey Lady, who floats around the building wearing a long grey dress and a lace cap, and at her waist hangs a large bunch of keys. Some believe her to be a member of the Bagot family, or possibly a senior servant. Another spectral lady is also seen here wearing darker clothes and a cape. An additional entity spotted on site, which, it is claimed, is definitely male, has been witnessed by staff looking out of a window on the first floor, appearing to twist a ring on his right hand; however, why he does this, no one is sure.

Playing sports, particularly archery, in the grounds of Blithfield Hall has been said to encourage the appearance of a small, spectral boy who is said to have fallen down a well in this area; one of the servants is said to have tried to catch him – sadly to no avail. Ever since, people have described hearing anguished screams that seem to reverberate as if from inside a well. This has to be a supernatural replay of the past, as the water hole was filled in many years ago. Other people have also described the shade of a man who stands wringing his hands. Could this be the servant who attempted to save the lad?

Bradnop

Bradnop is the location where a Jacobite soldier was murdered by one of his own comrades. Legend has it that his faithful hound was also put to the sword whilst trying to save his master. The site at which this deed had been done was reported as being behind Oxhay Farm. Thenceforth a large phantom black dog, known to some as Blackstock, began to haunt the area, loudly howling and growling. One can only imagine that he is still looking to avenge his master's demise. It would seem that he has no trust of anyone and is very aggressive to those unlucky enough to see him.

Brereton

Rumoured to be haunted by a black dog with large pointed ears and glowing eyes, Brereton's spooky reputation has evoked fear and fascination among many for years. One witness described the hound as looking like a Belgian Shepherd dog, and two young girls once asked their parents who the 'big black wolf' with 'big white teeth'

An artist's impression of a typical Grey Lady.

was. One witness who saw the dog says that right behind it crashed a large ball of white light that seemed to shatter into slithers of light, while at the same moment the ghostly hound vanished from sight. Local man Tom Smith claims to have seen the black dog on several occasions, but, in his opinion, it was a friendly creature and if it was a ghost it only had good intentions. He also claims that on one occasion it was actually watching over him as some rather unsavoury characters were walking behind him.

On the A51, between Brereton and Rugeley, is the site of Ravenhill House, which was at one time a temporary hospital provided for British soldiers during the First World War. One of my correspondents wrote to me a number of years ago, and told a story about seeing the spectre of a lovely, friendly and helpful nurse dressed in an old-fashioned uniform, who seemed to pop in and out of many of the rooms, simply carrying on her duties as if still living.

Some claim to have seen an old lady kneeling or sitting while staring into an old-fashioned fireplace; this vision only appears very fleetingly before she dissolves into thin air. Walkers and ramblers in the area have described the sound of invisible horses galloping by and the wheels you would have heard on an old-fashioned coach – but nothing is to be seen.

Barry Jackson told me that while driving to Brereton from Rugeley, he had stopped for a moment and, getting out of the vehicle, heard someone shout the words 'Halt! Who goes there?' Yet no one at all was to be seen that could have made such a challenge. Barry believes, therefore, that it must surely have been a ghostly voice calling out.

Barry Leason had an unusual experience while driving through the village of Brocton. He had been for a meal in the nearby village of Milford, when he realised there was a puncture in one of his rear tyres. He was even more angry when he realised the spare wheel in his boot was flat and, to make matters even worse, neither he or his girlfriend had brought their mobile phones with them that night, having previously decided that for once they would not be disturbed by anything.

Moaning loudly, Barry walked back into the village and saw an old-fashioned red telephone box. Delighted, he made his way towards it, entered the box and picked up the receiver, only to hear on the other end the sound of a woman crying. He hung up the phone in case it was a crossed line and tried again, but once again the sound was still to be heard. Perhaps even more strange was the overpowering smell of perfume, which he immediately recognised as the fragrance of Poison, which was popular at the time. Thinking that coincidences happened, he finally managed to get through to his father and explain what had happened. His dad told him to stay where he was and that he would come out to them with a

The haunted telephone box, Brocton.

spare tyre. Returning to the car, he saw that his girlfriend was very upset; she claimed that she had seen a crying woman of about thirty years of age, who had banged on the car door before simply vanishing from sight. Did this experience link in some way to the experience that Barry had in the telephone box? One would surely think that it was far too much of a coincidence to be anything else.

lodge, before suddenly disappearing. Other people have reported the sound of wind howling around them even on the mildest of days, and David Thompson tells me that on one occasion he saw a kite flying with a line reaching to the ground but with no one present to hold it. Thinking he would get what appeared to be a freebie, when he reached the area neither line nor kite was present. Poor David was very disappointed and rather spooked as well!

Brocton Hall

Brocton Hall plays host to an unusual haunting. A lady of fairly modern appearance, wearing a mac, the sort that was popular in the fifties and sixties, has been spotted, making her way towards the golf

Brough Park

The park is said to be haunted by several ghosts. One particularly alarming report concerns a young man who heard the sound of what he described as a dog being choked, perhaps on a chain or rope. Focusing his vision, he saw in the distance a man and dog walking towards him. Then, in the blink of an eye, they disappeared from sight. When telling his story, he was informed of the ghost of a Roman soldier, who was regularly seen with a large black dog. Another person, while walking down a path known as Dickie's Gutter towards a garden of remembrance, came upon what he described as an incredibly pretty girl sitting on the ground and leaning against an old sandstone wall. The man described her as being of gypsy-type appearance with long, black, curly hair down to her waist, and high boots crossed with laces. The man turned to the girl to say hello, but immediately felt his feet locked to the ground and at that very moment a silver coin fell from his top pocket. The man had been searching for coins with a metal detector and thought it had been a lucky day when he'd found an old silver coin. He reached down to pick the coin up and was intending to introduce himself to the young woman, but unfortunately it was not such a lucky day after all – both the coin and the girl suddenly vanished from sight.

An artist's impression of the Romany girl.

Brownhills

Not all ghost stories are old stories; in fact, I often find the newer ones far more interesting. Jim Davis told me of a strange experience he had early one morning while preparing his stall on Brownhills Market. It was dawn and Jim thought it was unusual that a young woman should to be walking around the market area and looking at stalls that didn't have anything on them at that time, just the steel frameworks. At a distance, she appeared to be quite normal and solid, an attractive girl with long brown hair. As she came closer to Jim's stall, however, it became clear to him that she was floating just off the floor, rather than walking. She then floated further on out of the market and disappeared from view. Jim made enquiries around the area, and was told that the ghost of the girl had been seen by several people before and that they felt she was someone who used to visit the market but had suddenly passed away. It seems her spirit likes to return on occasions.

Brooklands Road, Brownhills

Janet told me that about eight years ago her daughter moved into what used to be a miner's cottage in Brooklands Road in Walsall Wood, just outside Brownhills. When Janet went to stay, her daughter would give her the front bedroom to sleep in. Janet claims that she saw a woman bending over the bed and tucking in the bedclothes, as though she were tucking a child up in bed.

Apparently, on another occasion, she saw someone come out of the back bedroom, jump across the landing and into the front room. Janet says her daughter's dog would often sit at the bottom of the bed watching something and growling. As we all know, animals tend to be very perceptive to otherwordly phenomena, so perhaps he could see the same things that Janet had.

Burntwood

It is here that an exceptionally tall man with a large black dog has been seen walking across the roads, often in front of oncoming vehicles, before simply dissolving into thin air. No one knows for sure who or what this ghost is, but some locals believe it may be a haunting that relates to an accident that happened many years ago on the road halfway between Burntwood and Woodhouses, in the area of Burntwood hospital.

Emmanuel Road, Burntwood

Janet told me that when she lived in Emmanuel Road in Burntwood about fifty years ago, somebody would knock on the doors and ring the bells along the row of houses in the street late at night and in the early hours of the morning. This happened on a regular basis and everyone in the row thought it must be children playing around, until they exchanged stories with one another. They then realised that when each of them had gone to the door, no one would be in sight, and that these occurrences happened at a time of night when children were most unlikely to be out and about. One of the neighbours asked a psychic to see what she could make of it. She said that a young man had been very seriously injured on a motorbike in that area and felt that the door knocking and bell ring was something to do with this incident.

St John the Baptist Church, Burslem

St John the Baptist Church has a very unusual story of a ghostly nature. It concerns a lady known as the local witch, Molly Leigh, who resided in an area known as Hamil Grange, hidden by trees and thick woodland. Legend has it that Molly was not the prettiest of girls, and that her looks may even have turned the milk she sold to make a living. She also kept a blackbird that had been tamed and could mimic all the birds of the forest, as well as human voices. Molly was not admired by some members of St John's Church, including Revd Spencer. The local pub, The Turk's Head, equally objected to the wise woman, claiming Molly was to blame when bad beer was served.

When Molly died in 1746, legend has it that most, though not all, were pleased to see her demise. It was believed that she had jewellery and coins stored in her cottage that had been given to her as gifts and after the Revd Spencer conducted her funeral, in the company of others, he decided to check out her cottage for any paraphernalia or objects that needed removing or perhaps destroying. Revd Spencer instructed the group to stand back as he entered the building, but he returned just as quickly, screaming that Molly was sitting in a chair by the fireside and had mumbled words that shook him to the bone.

Three other clergymen were called in. They made their way to the churchyard and, under the light of candles, opened the grave and performed a religious exorcism. Legend has it that whatever happened here, the reverend's three clerical comrades fled the scene, leaving him to finish the deed himself. He had with him Molly's blackbird imprisoned in a cage, which protested throughout the ceremony. When he had finished, he put the bird into the coffin and closed the lid, and everyone assumed that would be the end of the matter. However, from that time onwards people have spoken of a little blackbird that hops around the churchyard, unusual whistles and high-pitched voices, and of a lady that occasionally visits her graveside but vanishes just as quickly.

For many years after her death, the young people of the village would play a little game where they would chant, 'Molly Leigh, follow me. Molly Leigh, follow me.' And some claim that she did! The tomb of Molly Leigh is in the south side of St John the Baptist Church. As for the blackbird – well, who knows where it may flit and fly!

Burslem

There is an interesting ghost story that concerns the main street of Burslem, where many good witnesses have reported seeing a lady carrying a bucket and, on other occasions, with a milk pail on her head. In 1976, Jenny Moreton saw the lady and asked if she was alright. Apparently she replied, 'Not to worry missus – it's only me, Molly. But I'm sorry if I've disturbed you,' and proceeded to walk on down the road. This is a surprising story because a little research suggests this lady's spirit was exorcised by clergymen many years before. Jenny Moreton says she seemed a friendly soul if not, in her words, 'a little loopy'. During the 1970s, a similar looking figure had also been reported moving very quickly around the churchyard in Burslem, but with neither bucket nor milk pail.

A Trick of the Eyes in Burton-on-Trent

Not all ghost stories come from times of old, and the following case is a perfect example. In the marketplace area, some council men were working on a job they had been sent to. It was quite early in the morning and few people were around, when suddenly past them walked an extremely pretty girl of about eighteen or nineteen in a very short skirt and boots which would probably have been the typical attire of your typical 1960s 'dolly bird'. As the foreman was not there at the time, the three men wolf-whistled and shouted to her. She turned round, smiled at them, then walked on a few more feet before simply dissolving into thin air. The lads were so shocked by this that they stopped the job and refused to start again until the foreman returned. The foreman did not believe their story, instead telling the men to show more respect when a lady walked by the next time.

Phantom Footsteps in Burton-on-Trent

The streets of Burton have their fair share of paranormal activity and would probably make an excellent site for a ghost walk. Around 1998, John had a strange experience in Station Street, in the place that had once been the old Bass site. He heard footsteps behind him, like a clicking sound that perhaps you would hear from a lady walking in high-heels. When he stopped and looked behind him, there was no one in sight, and the footsteps stopped abruptly. The minute he continued walking, however, the clicking started again. Not an easily frightened man, John stopped and asked what was going on. Hearing no more, he briskly made his way home and nothing more was heard of the strange high-heel clicks. Clearly he must have scared off whatever it was that was causing the noise!

3
Creepy Goings-on in Cannock

THE Castle Ring is an area that has had human habitation from around 50 AD and was believed to be the home of the ancient Cornovii Celtic tribe. Although the expert eye can still pick up the perimeter earthworks, not much is visible today, but there is no doubt farming would have taken place at different times throughout history here, and also hunting when a hunting lodge stood on the north-west side. Close examination of the land shows there are still indications of ploughing having taken place to the south-east of the area, and some remains have been found of items that would have been used at the hunting lodge. It has always had a history of being a place of paranormal activity and the appearance of ghosts.

In the days before the woods of Cannock Chase and its ancient forest enclosed this site, legend had it that people could look out and see four different parts of the country, or counties as we refer to them today, as Castle Ring has a vantage point that is the very highest in the Midlands.

People came here for two reasons; firstly, it was a secure place to avoid attacks from other tribes and, secondly, it also had quite large supplies of flint that could be made use of. Castle Ring has certainly been described over the years as being one of the most energised places to visit. People often travel here from paranormal organisations and often report the same sightings, such as the tall black figures that are said to appear in the centre of the ring, and people dressed from head to toe in white, again in the centre of the ring. This is claimed to happen during the hours of darkness and in broad daylight too. Claims have also been made of hearing chanting, humming and unusual singing, and also the sound of drumming or the hammering of stone on stone. This would certainly fit in with the type of people who would have inhabited Castle Ring in the past and if it is their ghosts or spirits that return, we are witnessing shades of yesteryear or perhaps replays of the past.

It is also an area that is favoured by people interested in UFOs and aliens, and it is claimed this is one of the best places to look for such things in Staffordshire. Perhaps stranger still, are the reports of

One of the many roads that lead to Cannock Chase.

pumas, black wolves and other unusual creatures in the area, including apes or Bigfoot-type entities. The area has had so many reports of strange goings-on over the years that one local newspaper started up their own Cannock Chase X-File reports, and seemed to have no shortage of people wishing to get involved or reporting the most incredible cases to them.

An interesting thing to note, and something that may explain the ragged characters seen close by Castle Ring, are the reports that a long time ago, when the fort stood proud here, the deceased were buried in a nearby area which some believe is where Gentleshaw Church stands – very close to the Ring. Other stories involve the ghosts of very young people, described as 'the children of the mill', which once stood at Cannock Chase, and also the regular manifestation of the so-called Sad Nun of Nunswell.

Four Crosses Inn, Cannock

This public house has long had a history of being haunted. My good friend Edward Ward, known as Mystic Ed, an excellent local medium and psychic, was called to investigate this building in 2005 after reports were received of the fireplace self-lighting and happily burning away, despite no human hands, and glasses that smashed and flew around the building of their own accord. Ed felt that a spirit who had been an alcoholic, with the nickname Charlie the Drunkard, was to blame for much of the activity, and also that the building was home to the ghost of a middle-aged woman, a soldier, and a young boy named Scottie present. Much of what Ed picked up was supported by people who had seen or experienced things that fitted in with this report.

A fire starting by itself in a fireplace is an unusual and somewhat puzzling phenomenon but one that was experienced by my own mother and her sister many years ago following the death of their aunt. It had been a very harsh winter and coal was in short supply. Visiting their late aunt's cottage, they decided they would collect a couple of bags of coal and take it home. My mother had no doubt that her aunt would not have minded this. However, after making their way through the freezing cold house and going into the cellar to collect the coal, they were more than a little scared when coming back out of the cellar to see a fire in the fireplace blazing away in the living room. All the doors were locked and only they had entered the house. My mother was, without a shadow of a doubt, one of the finest mediums in the UK, but even she was alarmed by

A black puma is said to have been spotted on Cannock Chase.

this. Together with her sister, they swiftly dropped the coal and left the building in a great hurry!

Laburnan Road, Cannock

For several years, I worked as a college lecturer in Cannock and came to the conclusion that it is one of those places in the world one could call it a portal, where energies from the other side seem to come through easily. Laburnum Road is a perfectly ordinary place of residence, and yet during the 1950s, '60s and '70s, people claim to have regularly seen the ghost of a man described as being around thirty years of age, powerful and robust, with thick, black slicked-back hair, trying to climb into the bedrooms of teenagers' houses. This is said to be something that went on for over thirty years. Research seems to come up with little to prove this to be entirely true, and one wonders if it may be more relevant to an urban myth that has grown by word of mouth. Yet for all that, good independent witnesses claim it to be a true story.

Phantom Aircrafts in Cannock

A very unusual ghost story was told by a gentleman in 2000. As he sat relaxing in his living room, he suddenly heard the drone of what sounded like an aircraft in trouble in the distance. Going outside to investigate, he saw what looked like an old-fashioned aircraft coming closer and closer and that other people in the area were also looking and pointing to the sky. As the plane got closer, it started to fly incredibly low, and

the sound of its engines were quite deafening. One old man shouted to the others, 'I know that sound – it's a Wellington bomber!'

Within seconds the skies had cleared and the air fell silent – not even a bird was to be heard. Did these people witness the replay of something that had happened many decades earlier? Is there a historical link to this area of Cannock with a Wellington Bomber? No one can say for sure, but the ghost of an aeroplane in the sky is not as unusual as one might think; numerous cases of spectral aircraft have been reported across the world.

Cannock College

The college in the town is reportedly a very haunted building. While working there as a lecturer, several members of staff told me of seeing strange figures in a mist that appeared to be wearing fairly modern dress, and possibly looked like they were teenagers.

Some of the security staff told me of hearing the sounds of heavy footsteps on the stairs, and loud bangs when the building should have been empty. People also speak of a figure that stands at the front of the college, seemingly welcoming people into the building. He is only seen in the twinkling of an eye, but appears very solid and real before completely disappearing. People walking past the college have also heard the sounds of music in the early hours, when certainly no one would be inside.

One of the most haunted parts of the college is the so-called White House, where quite a few of the admin staff work in a

The author at Cannock College.

Cannock College.

The White House by Cannock College.

collection of small rooms. I was once part of a paranormal team that investigated this building and the group I was with came up with several ghosts, including a lady they called Elizabeth, and three others named Mary, Little Ellen and John. We also recorded some very unusual noises on tape, which included male and female voices that did not belong to any of the group investigating the college that evening. Again, college staff who have worked in this part of the building in the past feel sure it is haunted or at least visited by spirit energies.

Walsall Road, Cannock

A very unusual experience happened to a local bobby some years ago outside the cinema in Walsall Road and neighbouring music shop. As the policeman reached that area he would hear the sound of a 1960s-type Vespa or Lambretta scooter, which was popular with riders, particularly those who followed the Mod fashion in the '60s. It would pull up right outside the cinema, but was far enough ahead of the policeman for him not to be able to reach it and have a little word with the rider. This seemed to happen regularly over a three-week period and then nothing further would be seen or heard for a while.

Other people around Cannock centre also tell of hearing a scooter and, when looking round, nothing would be there. This is a story that is of particular interest to me because it is one I have experienced personally. A little research suggests it may be the ghost of a lad who was killed on a scooter nearby, but no one seems to know for sure when it happened or who the young man was.

Cannock Library

Hawks Green Lane, Cannock

The town's library is very up-to-the-minute in style and operation. Apparently, however, the building does have two ghosts – a lady who is said to walk along the length of the rooms and leaves behind a strong smelling perfume, and Joe, who was described as a most diligent caretaker in his lifetime, and who can still become very cross if everything is not as it should be, or if there is talking going on in the library! There are also some very unusual sounds when the building is empty, and a lady's voice saying 'Shh!' when there are people in the building.

Hawks Green Lane is said to have regular apparitions of horses and riders, particularly on Sunday afternoons. Many have reported hearing the sound of horses and people, always describing it as a very happy sound, including laughter. However, although laughter is *heard*, rarely is anything *seen*.

At one time there had been a successful and popular riding school here that provided training for pupils at very reasonable costs, meaning that working-class kids as well as the well-to-do could afford to learn to ride. Perhaps this is just a ghostly replay of those times. Other people claim to have seen a large white horse and a brown horse walking one

The author outside the White House offices.

Electric Palace Picture House, Cannock.

The author outside the Electric Palace Picture House, Cannock.

Cannock New Library.

behind the other, who simply dissolve from sight before you reach them.

The Prince of Wales Centre, Cannock

Like many theatres, this one has its fair share of ghosts, with reports of unusual sounds and noises and unexplained fragrances that seem to float through the air from no apparent source, particularly the smell of lavender and Parma violets. The Prince of Wales is my favourite theatre and not only have I appeared there with my clairvoyance show on several occasions, but it is somewhere I like to go to see other shows too when I possibly can.

Jim, the Commissionaire, has become a good friend over the years and told me the story of the fireman seen at the rear of the building at times, yet investigation proves there has not been such a person in the area. Researching the history of the building, it transpires that at one time this was where Cannock Fire Station operated from, so perhaps the fireman is a shade from another time or a spirit returning occasionally to check that everything is in order.

I had a very strange experience at the theatre whilst giving one of my demonstrations of clairvoyance on stage. We had a very big audience that evening and my support medium was my good friend from Birmingham, John Routley. John did the first half of the show, then I came on to do the second half. Right at the end of the show it is not unusual for me to sing a song, often an Elvis Presley song (I'm a massive fan).

At the end of this particular show, as I was singing American Trilogy, John had joined me on stage but stood back a little way while I performed. During the song,

The author at the Prince of Wales Centre.

it is common for me to turn round with my back to the audience and, as I did this, I noticed that John was looking at me with a puzzled expression on his face. That night I had worn a white stage suit, but John later insisted that there were two people in white suits, not just me on stage, and he felt the presence of Elvis was there with me.

I was very surprised when two ladies who had been in the audience asked me who the man in the white suit was standing beside me as I was singing. It certainly wasn't John, for he was wearing dark-coloured clothes and had moved towards the back of the stage, so it would seem the ladies confirmed what John had already told me.

Strangely enough, this experience repeated itself some years later. As some of you may know, every Monday night I have my own radio show on Wolverhampton City Radio, WCR 101.8 FM, called 'Philip Solomon's Music and Memories', and I am very lucky every week to be able to interview celebrities. On one occasion I was interviewing Sonny West, Elvis's personal bodyguard and close friend, by telephone to America. It was a fascinating interview and Sonny spoke very well and quite emotionally at times about his late, great friend. In the studio my producer sits across the desk from me, so we can make sure the show runs smoothly.

During the interview I noticed that he was looking rather perturbed and after the interview he said to me, 'I'm sure there's an answer to this and perhaps it was my imagination, but while you were interviewing Sonny, there was like a strange white mist and the faint outline of a man in a white suit standing by you.'

The Prince of Wales Centre.

The author on the set of his radio show.

Elvis Solomon: the author in costume after a clairvoyance show.

I have to tell you that my producer is also a scientist who does not believe in the occurrence of supernatural events, or, at the very least, would go about looking for a logical answer to such things. In this instance, and in the infamous words of Elvis Presley, he was left all shook up!

The Bell Inn, Cannock

About ten years ago, Janet had a strange experience at the Bell Inn, which is situated in Watling Street on the A5. Many years ago it was a coaching inn but is now what is known as a 'Ham and Eggs Pub'. She had never felt comfortable sitting at the one end of the pub, but on this particular occasion it was crowded and she didn't have any choice.

She says that she always seems to get a funny premonition-like feeling, and, on this occasion, she knew something was about to happen. Sure enough, before her eyes she saw four or five men dressed like Cavaliers walk straight through a solid wall. They then sat down and had a drink, and, when finished, walked back *through* the wall. Speaking to the landlord about her experience, he showed her a very old plan of the building, which showed that at one time there had been doors where she saw the men enter and depart.

Janet says she also saw a group of what looked like Roman soldiers, who came through one end of the building and marched out through the other end. She got the impression that they were not aware of the people around them nor the building that they had just walked through. This makes sense as the inn would not have existed there at that period in time.

Cannock Chase

In the heart of Staffordshire is the beautiful Cannock Chase, a densely wooded area of great beauty where many strange things have been seen. Notably, in 2007, the *Staffordshire Post* newspaper ran a most interesting story about a number of people who had seen entities that resembled werewolves on the Chase, many being spotted close to the German War Cemetery. Apparently, one witness, when riding his motorcycle, saw a creature stand up on its hind legs and run away into the woods. Another man in a vehicle had a similar experience, witnessing a werewolf-like creature that he said raised itself up to possibly seven feet in height.

Perhaps an unusual addition to this story is that in more recent years, particularly around the area of the German War Cemetery, people have found large

The German War Cemetery, where it is said one can sometimes see the apparition of a werewolf-like creature.

animals such as deer mutilated and killed in a very unusual way. Perhaps this belongs to the field of cryptology, or could they have witnessed the ghost of something that walked in our world thousands of years ago? Or are there really werewolves on Cannock Chase? Anything, in my experience, is possible until proven otherwise.

Extraterrestrial Spectres of Cannock Chase

The area has long played host to a series of rumours concerning extraterrestrial entities. A mysterious apparition was seen by a local woman and has since been nicknamed 'the Lady of The Chase'. The woman in question was driving across Cannock

Chase after visiting a friend who lived in Cannock when she saw the ghost lady. It was about 11.30 p.m. at night and she had taken a shorter route across the Chase known as Spring Slade Lodge, when she had to slam her brakes on to avoid hitting a person in front of her on the road. Terribly shocked but gathering her wits, she saw in her headlights a very tall female form who appeared to be quite grey, completely naked, and devoid of either breasts or genitalia. The woman was particularly drawn to the figure's large, hypnotic eyes, which were fixed upon her and caused her to freeze for a moment, completely unable to even move a muscle. After a short period, the figure turned and walked away into the dark forest.

The driver clearly felt this being was female, yet wasn't sure exactly what she was seeing and, as soon as she could, accelerated away and left the area as quickly as she could! With all the reports of UFOs and other strange activity, one wonders if she had seen an alien from another planet. Or was it quite simply a ghost? Perhaps the reason the body was not formed was that the replay may have weakened over the years.

In 2003, more terrifying and unexplained occurrences were reported, but this time it was of a monster from the waters. Police were called to investigate a pool in Roman View, Church Bridge, Cannock, where several people claimed to have seen a crocodile or alligator. These were reli-

Cannock Chase.

41

Waters often hold ghost stories; could this lake play host to the apparition of a large, prehistoric fish?

The Spectre of Lady Harriet

Upon Cannock Chase you will find the beautiful Shugborough Hall, which, like all historical buildings, has its share of paranormal activity. The smell of fragrances from unknown sources, things that go bump in the night and objects that seem to move position have all been reported. But Shugborough also has what can only be described as a rather nice haunting – the ghost of the good Lady Harriet. Never seen but on certain occasions known to knock gently on doors, it is said that when she moves away, one hears the sound of her silk dress rustling on the floor. Almost everyone says that Lady Harriet's ghost brings a feeling of calm and happiness and is not at all scary, unless you are of a naturally nervous disposition.

The Mysterious Ape-Like Creature

There has long been a history of reported sightings of a creature that looks either like a gorilla or large monkey or something from another world. Far too many people have reported seeing this for it to be dismissed, and in fact it is something I have witnessed in the company of other people too. Of course it doesn't necessarily mean it is a creature that is living on The Chase; it could be the ghost of an ape that had perhaps escaped at some time in the past and died there, perhaps under terrifying circumstances. This could certainly imprint and cause a replay to be seen by those of a sensitive nature. Strangely enough, one of the group members with me on the

able witnesses and the police were joined by RSPCA inspectors and other animal experts, who, after great investigation, could find no sign of such a creature in the pool or surrounding areas. They suggested, however, that it might be a huge fish, such as a carp, which apparently can look rather like a croc or alligator, but locals were not convinced and considered this suggestion to be ridiculous. It is possible that the creature had escaped from a private zoo, but one would wonder how such a creature could survive our harsh winters.

One person even alleged that, whilst watching two swans and a line of cygnets, there was a terrible commotion in the water and they clearly saw a creature in excess of five feet long with a tail that must have been another two feet long with a flat head. One has to say that the description doesn't really sound like any fish you could think of. Reports seem to have quietened now, but could it have been a projection of something that had lived in this world many thousands of years ago?

evening we witnessed this creature was adamant that what we had seen was more like a bear and that, as it moved away from us, was dragging what looked like a chain behind it.

Many other people have seen similar things on Cannock Chase and one can never be sure that it was not perhaps someone dressed in a monkey outfit, but you can't argue with what you have seen with your own eyes; far too many people have reported similar sights for such a long time that there has to be some truth in it, one would think. A few months before this book was written, Jane contacted me to say that as she drove across The Chase in the early hours with her daughter, a similar creature had walked across the road in front of her and she had to swerve her car to avoid hitting it.

Cannock Chase.

A Faceless Entity

About fifteen years ago, Nigel Barratt from Wimblebury says he had been to Skegness with his trailer to pick up a friend's car, who did stock car racing. Arriving back in Wandon, which is between Rugeley and Hazel Slade, at about three o'clock in the morning, he saw a woman standing on the side of the road dressed in a short grey jacket and long grey skirt. She had shoulder-length black hair but her face seemed to have no features, appearing rather as a grey blob.

The woman stepped in front of his car as he approached and, naturally, he slammed on the brakes, but the car just went straight through her. Shaken by what had just happened, Nigel jumped out of the vehicle to check that she was alright, but there was no one to be seen. Although this happened in late August and it was quite a warm night, the atmosphere was freezing cold and eerily silent; there was absolutely no sound to be heard. Nigel says he cannot explain what he had seen that night and when he took his dogs for a walk in the area about a month later, they just sat down, refusing to move on.

Nigel says there have also been some odd things happening in his house in recent times, such as seeing one of his dogs that had passed on out of the corner of his eye, lying in his bed. His wife also claims that when they were in bed one night, she saw an old lady with silver hair in a rocking chair; the apparition moved closer and closer towards her until she actually felt the woman brush against her face, and, when she tried to wake Nigel, she found that she was so scared she couldn't move or speak!

Nigel has since discovered that the spirit was that of a woman called Mrs Eden who used to reside in the house.

On another occasion, their son saw a man dressed in black with a tall hat lying on his bed for a split second, before he disappeared, creepily leaving an imprint in the bedclothes. Nigel's father-in-law thinks the description sounds like his wife's great-grandfather. On another occasion, a doll's house belonging to their granddaughter fell over for no apparent reason. Nigel says all these things seem to occur without fail around October time, which is the anniversary of his father's death about five years ago.

The Tree with No Leaves, Cannock Chase

A young couple from Hednesford spent much of their time on Cannock Chase when they were courting, particularly favouring to sit together under a lovely old leaf-laden oak tree. The young lady's parents originally objected to their relationship, for her beau was known to enjoy poaching on the Chase. However, a wedding date was agreed when he promised to give up his rabbit-catching days once and for all.

As the wedding day approached, legend has it that the young man was goaded into one final poaching venture on the Chase by his close friends. But that night was not a good night for poaching, for they were caught by the gamekeeper who recognised the lads, and in fear of being apprehended, one of them stepped forward and discharged his shotgun, mortally wounding the gamekeeper. The young

Cannock Chase, where ghostly apparitions have been sighted.

man who was to be married had a good heart and could not leave the dying man as the others fled the scene. Unfortunately, this meant he was apprehended, accused of the crime and ultimately he swung by the neck until he was dead for a crime he had not committed.

On the day of his execution, his bride-to-be made her way to their special tree and noted that not a leaf was to be seen on it. Legend tells us that when she saw the leafless tree, she took it to be a symbol that life was to come to an end for her and she drowned herself that very day. Legend also has it that to this day this particular tree never grows a leaf and mourns the untimely death of its two young lovers.

People have reported seeing a ghostly couple, perhaps reunited in the other world, while their shades can be seen by us in this world when the energies and occasion are just right.

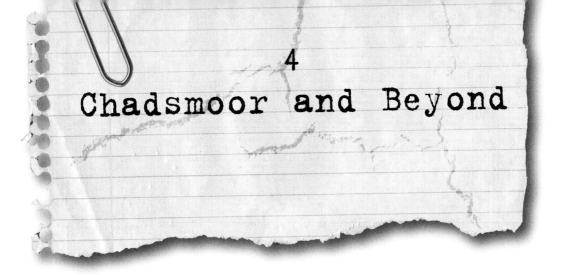

4
Chadsmoor and Beyond

A Poltergeist in Greenwood Avenue

Julie contacted me to tell me about when her then-pregnant daughter and her husband moved into their new home in Greenwood Avenue. Not long after they moved in, one of the neighbours asked her if she would like some furniture that had belonged to a family member who had passed away. This included two old-fashioned wardrobes and a kidney-shaped dressing table. As they hadn't had a chance to furnish much of the house at the time, they were grateful for the offer and it was duly delivered to their home shortly afterwards.

The furniture was placed in one of the bedrooms, and, not long afterwards, strange creaking and banging noises could sometimes be heard coming from the room. After Julie's daughter had her baby, she could still hear the creaks in the middle of the night when she got up to feed her baby, which seemed to be getting ever louder. By the time her brother-in-law came to visit for a few days, the creaking was a regular occurrence.

The first night he was there, he stayed in the bedroom where the furniture had been put. Julie's daughter and her husband didn't say anything to him about the noises, thinking it might alarm him, but a couple of hours after going to bed, he came into their room to wake them. He was going to sleep downstairs on the sofa as he couldn't get any rest because of the creaking and banging noises that seemed to be coming from the wardrobes, and a sound that was like a stick being dragged backwards and forwards against the sides of a child's cot. Shortly after this, their two sons came dashing into their room one night; they were absolutely terrified and were adamant that the wardrobes kept moving.

They decided enough was enough and chopped up the wardrobes and burned them in the back garden. Their next door neighbour saw the kidney-shaped dressing table outside the house and asked if she could have it. They said she could, but neglected to tell her about the strange events they'd been experiencing since the furniture came into their possession. Four or five weeks later, the neighbour told them she had taken it to one of the local charity shops as she was unnerved by the sudden emergence of strange banging and scratching noises in her house.

Chartley Moss Bog, near Stowe

There is a large peat bog to be found here that is over 100 acres in size and is a dangerous and spooky place to say the least. A top surface of peat 9ft thick floats on a large expanse of water, which is claimed to be more than 50ft deep. It is here that the ghost of a huntsman and his pack of beagles ride to the hunt. For hundreds of years, people have vanished or been lost here and many unusual experiences have occurred. The place itself is now not allowed to receive visitors without the permission of the owners and people are advised not to visit either on their own or in small groups. This is one place you would not wish to hear the sound of the hunter's horn in the morning.

Checkley

In the past it was rumoured to be difficult to employ gravediggers for Checkley churchyard. Obviously, this was an occupation that would require a man to go to the graveyard alone at first light and prepare a grave to receive a coffin later on that day. Those who fulfilled this role often said they felt uneasy, almost as if they were being watched, as they dug up the soil. People would claim that although the churchyard was a mostly pleasant place during the day, at night the atmosphere changed dramatically. Several people have reported seeing the figure of a monk, believed to be the ghost of Thomas Chawney, the final abbot of Croxden, whose abbey was destroyed during the Dissolution and the land and all other relevant properties were transferred to one Geoffrey Foljambe. Strangely enough, Abbot Chawney is buried next to the graves of the Foljambe family. But perhaps he was uncomfortable in this placement and this is the reason that he returns and watches where other people are to be buried. Other hauntings of the churchyard are said to include a small white dog. Its spectral state was confirmed when one lady saw it run straight through a solid wall. Is there a link between the bishop and the dog?

Chell

Westcliffe Hospital is said to have several resident ghosts, including a tall lady in blue and a gentleman wearing uniform, possibly a former employee of the hospital. Some of the residents who live in the new houses opposite have reported unusual sounds and figures in the gardens and some have suggested the houses have been built on the site of some old paupers' graves, (these were people who could not afford a proper funeral and were buried together in a very simple manner).

Church Eaton

Close to the Shropshire Union Canal comes an unusual sighting of an American airman who some believe crashed close to this site during the Second World War. People have described the smell of burning and the sound of a man calling for help in an American accent.

Cobridge

Reports of a huge, spectral white rabbit on the road from Cobridge to Etruria just as darkness falls and in an area known locally as 'the grove' date back to the 1850s. People say that before they see the apparition of the rabbit, the scream of a young child is heard, followed by the rabbit emerging from the trees and running along a short route before vanishing. Legend has it that many years ago two young boys who had been friends fell out and ended up in a terrible fight, which resulted in the tragic death of one of the lads. Some believe the fight may have been over a few coins, or possibly a pet rabbit, and, if that is the case, I suppose one can see the significance that might project such a haunting. Others believe the rabbit may be the spirit of the young lad, but this is something I wouldn't consider to be likely.

Draycott

Quite close to Draycott you will find an area known as Slade Man's Hole. Legend suggests that at one time a great battle took place here. It is also claimed that if you chuck a stone against a rock here, a soldier from the other world will step forth before you. Could it be that a soldier was cut down here and buried on the spot? Why throwing a stone at a rock should bring forth his spirit, it is not known; perhaps he was put to death with a rock or stone rather than the slash of steel.

Draycott

One evening a number of years ago, a group of friends were making their way home after a work party around Christmas time. Four of them, plus the taxi driver, saw an elderly lady wearing white appear in the car's headlights. Another taxi carrying other partygoers travelling just behind them reported seeing the same woman, but said she was kneeling down in the road and praying. The incident happened on the road between Five Lanes and Six Lanes, very near to Draycott-in-the-Clay. The entire group worked for a medical organisation, and one of them was a nursing sister who had not been drinking that evening, but insisted the vehicles must stop so she could attend to the woman and check that she was alright. Unfortunately, the taxi driver was so scared by the experience that he flatly refused to stop and quickly drove on. The sister was shocked as she looked through the rear window; the old woman had disappeared and there was no one in sight.

Dresden

The area near Longton Park can be very quiet, especially at night. One correspondent told me that one time when he and his girlfriend were walking in the park past the bowling green by the lake, the shadow of a man crossed their pathway, twice! On another occasion, they also noticed strange lights at the top of the clock tower, yet on closer examination nothing and no one was to be seen.

Enville

A village of great historical interest very close to Kinver, Enville is certainly worthy of noting in this book. There are many stories that have been told before, but perhaps the most famous ghosts are that of a former lord and his lady appearing in and around Enville and sometimes walking on the nearby Kinver Edge. The story goes that the Earl of Enville had married a gypsy girl whom he loved greatly, and, despite opposition from members of his family, they had been incredibly happy and the people of Enville and Kinver had come to love the kind and generous Lady of Enville.

Further down the village, you will come across the site of the rectory. This building has had more than its share of paranormal activity. Today it has been turned into luxury flats, but, in the past, people would tell of seeing a foot-

The rectory at Enville.

man who walks across the road into the adjoining church, and in the gardens the spectre of an exceedingly pretty young girl dressed as you would expect an upstairs maid to have been dressed around 1780. There are also the remains of a stable where people claim to have heard the sounds of horses and coaches in the hours of darkness, when no one was around. The Cat public house also has its share of ghosts, including the vision of a lady in an apron, and glasses that rattle for no obvious reason.

At certain times of the year, the ghost of a small black boy is seen running through the centre of the village. At other times, the boy is seen in the surrounding fields of Enville, throwing his arms in the air as if he has won a race or achieved success for some reason at the end of his ghostly run.

There is also either a ghostly black dog, puma or other non-native cat that growls and makes awful canine-like sounds at night. People claim they have seen a black cat in and around Enville

An artist's impression of an earl and a gypsy.

and Kinver Edge and these reports are from the most respected of witnesses, including a senior former policeman.

Gladstone Pottery Museum

There have been a great deal of changes to this building over the years. In 1970, the Gladstone Works closed down and was on the verge of being demolished and lost forever. Luckily, finances were found to save the building and it remains intact to this day. The staff here have told of strange goings-on in the building. In the area known as the Doctor's House,

it has been reported that unexplained bangs and footsteps have occasionally been heard. The aroma of strange fragrances is not unusual on the stairs that lead to the gallery, and objects have been known to move of their own accord, particularly during the night. It is a place that has drawn the interest of the paranormal investigation fraternity and has been filmed for broadcast purposes by the *Most Haunted* television programme team.

The Potteries Museum and Art Gallery, Hanley

The Potteries Museum and Art Gallery is a fascinating place to visit and if you are particularly interested in china, it is a wonderful day out. But the staff will tell you that at times it can have a strange atmosphere. Objects moving of their own accord has been witnessed, and one or two people have even suggested that the Spitfire Gallery may be haunted by energies around the aeroplane. Security staff have reported things being moved around that particular area, and sometimes even finding the canopy open on the cockpit

of the plane. Also reported is the smell of what could arguably be a battle scene – a mixture of smoke, fumes, and so on. It is not my place to dismiss a report, but as this particular plane never saw active service, it seems an unusual one to say the least.

The Regent's Theatre, Hanley

Almost every theatre throughout Britain has its own ghost story to tell, but it is outside the Regent's Theatre that bizarre reports have been made since its reopening in 1999. The spectres of two ladies, seemingly from the 1950s, have been seen walking towards the theatre, but vanish before they enter it. The building is said to have its share of cold spots, loud bangs and other noises, and a lady who sits in on shows but always vanishes halfway through.

Hartshill Hospital

The hospital has long had a claim of being haunted. Many of the nursing staff who worked the long shifts claim that it was not unusual for an extra nurse to be working with them, and they would often describe an elderly lady with a matron-like manner but, strangely enough, she was very rarely seen by a patient. One male nurse became so unnerved by the regular appearance of what he described as an old lady with a grey face that he was unable to continue his employment there. Could it be that this spirit appeared to the young man more than anyone else because she had worked there at a time when male nurses were unheard of and was perhaps puzzled as to what he was doing there? Other people have described objects being moved and the sound of rustling, starched clothing.

Apparently, the spirit nurse rarely spoke, only putting in sporadic appearances, but on one occasion she did enquire of someone if everything was alright that night, in a well-spoken English accent. Turning round the person claimed no one was to be seen, but felt sure she had been addressed by the ghost of Hartshill Hospital and not a member of staff or a patient.

Hartshill Institute

This institution was made available in 1859 with the proviso that it would provide learning and leisure activities for local inhabitants. The patronage and funding are attributed to famous potter, Colin Minton Campbell. In more recent years, it has become a place where theatre workshops are carried out by the Newcastle Players. Now, and in the past, it has always been rumoured to be a haunted building. The mid-1960s were said to be a significant time for witnessing hauntings; the leader of the theatre company spoke of seeing a figure that apparently glided from the balcony area into the building next door. It has been suggested by a number of the current players that the ghost that walks the building today is Colin Minton Campbell, or perhaps an unnamed owner of the cottage building next door.

Hatherton Hall

A fine Staffordshire building, the former lord of the manor apparently still rules the roost. Many people have described seeing an exceptionally tall man dressed in a long cloak either walking through the building or seen at the front entrance. Strangely, no member of the family has ever seen this ghost, but others not of his lineage have. On one well-known occasion, an apparition of the lord appeared at a Christmas party at the hall. Legend has it that several partygoers had somehow obtained the lord's skull and were using it to drink beer from; however, as the clock struck twelve, his disapproving spectre appeared, dressed in full armour. The uncouth guests abruptly stopped drinking from the skull — clearly they were not expecting a shade of the lord to appear and reprimand them for their lack of decorum!

The Cross Keys, Hednesford

The Cross Keys is allegedly a haunted pub, and, although no one knows for sure, locals feel this is associated with Staffordshire's infamous serial poisoner, Dr Palmer.

Susan Tomlinson told me many years ago that those who were sensitive to paranormal occurrences would have a feeling of sickness just outside the building but, strangely enough, be perfectly fine when walking in or leaving the premises. This was something that she often sensed herself. Today it does not seem to have the same effect on the customers. Well, not at the moment at least!

Hednesford

Here we have a report from the Brindley Heath area of a headless female ghost. Some people think it may be the replay of a terrible murder that took place in 1919. Elizabeth Gaskin was twenty-three years of age and separated from her husband. She had received a note to meet him and left her baby with her mother before making her way to a pool close to the Cannock and Rugeley colliery offices, as arranged. It is confirmed she arrived at her destination because colliery officials saw her with her husband Thomas walking towards a nearby wood. Unfortunately, this is the last time she was seen alive. Reported missing by her mother, a search began and Elizabeth's body — disturbingly minus her head — was later recovered from the nearby pool. Obviously the chief suspect was her husband, which was confirmed when he confessed they had quarrelled after he suggested getting back together and that he had strangled her, before later returning to the scene to chop off her head. Thomas Gaskin was hung at Winson Green Prison, Birmingham, in 1919 for the crime after a plea of insanity was refused and the jury returned a verdict of guilty of murder.

The vision that is seen today may not actually be that of poor Elizabeth, but such a terrible crime can imprint into the ether: a replay of the image of the person killed, perhaps the person who did the deed, and sometimes sounds of an audible nature. Certainly locals describe this as an unpleasant place at times and feelings of great unease are often sensed here.

Hixon

Carol Arnall is an author who writes a lot of ghost stories locally and is very specific in the information she discusses. In one of her books, *Mysterious Happenings*, she tells the story of a gentleman who had been sent to a storehouse, which was part of his company's property at Hixon, to work on stocktaking duties for a short time. The building stood on the Second World War aerodrome site, in one of the hangars which was inaccessible to the general public (except through the gates, which were always securely locked after entrance). The gentleman and his colleagues were all working at some distance from one another, when one of the men asked why the other two kept calling out for him. They both denied having called out to him at all.

All three men could also occasionally hear the sound of footsteps on the hard concrete floors, which did not belong to any of them. They were obviously concerned about this, as they were in a secure building which no one else had access to without first obtaining a key from the management. Also, the men discovered that when they moved towards the footsteps, the sound abruptly ceased, but on returning to their duties, the footsteps could be heard once again. Finally, losing patience, one of the men shouted out, 'Who is it and what do you want?' The footsteps immediately stopped and, strangely, from that moment on were not heard again.

When the man in charge of locking up the hangar was shutting everything down later that evening, one of his workmates waited at the gate for him. Upon reaching his friend, he was informed that a Second World War airman in full uniform, right down to the long greatcoat the Air Force men wore, had walked straight up to him and asked him if he knew where all his friends were, as he was just returning after being on leave and had been looking everywhere for them but couldn't find them.

He was so real and solid in body that the workman had answered him explaining that there had been no Air Force staff on the site for a great many years and that he must be mistaken or confused. Turning round to beckon his colleagues over to confirm what he had said, he looked around again but the airman had simply vanished from sight. The men all agreed that they had witnessed something of a paranormal nature.

Many people often get mixed up and think a ghost and spirit are the same thing, which they are not. A ghost is generally a replay of something that has happened in the past, a situation that can be seen and viewed over and over by those capable of such experiences. But I think one can say with great certainty that if you witness and communicate with a 'ghost' then this is actually a spirit – the energy of someone that has gone to the other side, but for whatever reason has returned to the earth plane and who chooses to link and communicate with you.

Perhaps the conversation with the airman may have allowed him to join his friends and family on the other side.

The Wandering Jew, Ipstones

Many places have relayed the story of the Wandering Jew, but it is perhaps in the moorlands of northern Staffordshire that one ghost story of the Wandering Jew is of particular significance. Many years ago, in the 1600s, legend tells us a poorly disabled man lived in a little cottage close to Ipstones. Hearing three loud taps at his door one evening, he opened it to find a stranger stood before him, a man of Jewish appearance who was wearing a long gown. The stranger asked if he might be allowed a drink. The disabled man replied that he was, but because of the difficulties he had in standing and walking, asked if he would like to help himself and also partake of a jug of ale.

The Jewish man thanked him greatly and then enquired how long he had been afflicted with the lameness that so hindered his movements. He replied, 'I have been this way for many, many years, Sir.' The Jewish man stopped drinking and took three leaves from his gown, which he put into the remains of the ale they had been drinking. He then topped the jug to its rim

with more ale and told the afflicted man to drink it over a three-week period and that it would not go flat or lose its taste. He also told him that he must praise and serve God with all his heart. The old man followed the Jew's instructions and within three weeks found himself in good health and, indeed, it is said he praised and spread the word of God for the rest of his life.

There are many other versions of the story of the Wandering Jew, but all seem to refer in one way or another to when Jesus made his way to Calvary carrying his cross for his own crucifixion. Jesus is said to have asked Ahasuerus, a Jew himself, for a little water. Another story says he asked a Jewish person if he might rest in his gateway; apparently both requests were refused, and Ahasuerus was henceforth cursed to wander the earth until the second coming of Christ. An unusual addition to this story is that the age of the Wandering Jew seems to change. Every time someone sees him, he is seen at different ages, but once someone has seen him at the age of 100 it seems he returns to the age of thirty, which is the age he was supposed to have been at the time of the crucifixion.

There is also the legend that if you refuse a drink of water, ale or beer to anyone in need, great ill fortune will come your way. Also, you are greatly advised not to ask the age of the Wandering Jew, for this is one of his great mysteries and although he may look somewhere between thirty and 100, of course he is well over 2011 years old, at the very least!

Ipstones Edge

The Revd F. Brighton told a most interesting story in one of his books of a spinney close to the Red Lion at Ipstones Edge. A young woman had been brutally murdered close to this site and her remains were buried there. Her corpse may never have been found were it not for the terrible nightmares her mother suffered, which revealed what had happened and where. From that time forth reports have come forward of people seeing someone standing over a bicycle, yet when approached, the vision dissolves before their eyes. Revd Brighton also relates a story from the First World War of an old farmhouse called The Hermitage, which was thus named because a miser at one time lived there and hoarded his wealth within it. Reports were made of an elderly, hunchbacked man, bent over, with a large hat who haunted the building. Those who visited the premises reported unusual noises and felt a wind that rushed past them. Unearthly screams and the sound of an organ being played were also heard. Apparently, a large spectral dog guarded the building, appearing on one occasion to a brave man who gave it a firm kick and found his foot travelling through something that was neither solid or of this world!

Ipstones Churchyard

The churchyard has long had a history of being haunted, but one of its more unusual hauntings is a disembodied voice that speaks or whispers in a foreign language into the ear of unsuspecting visitors. There is also a stone close to Ipstones that is known as Horseley's Stone, which is said to be visited by the ghost or spirit of a little bird that is thought to be an omen for good luck to those sensitive enough to see it.

Keele Hall

Keele Hall was built in around 1580 and at one time was the home of the Grand Duke, Michael of Russia. People who have seen a vision here believe it to be this gentleman. Others have seen a maid dressed in Victorian attire, or caught a glimpse in their peripheral vision of what appears to be a doorway, which, on closer inspection, is nothing of the sort. Of course, many old buildings have had passages and doorways bricked up and plastered over and it is possible that sensitive people could be picking up a replay of yesteryear or indeed tuning into the history of the building itself.

Kidsgrove

Rumoured to be the regular haunting place of the Bogart, there are several stories that abound about this particular haunting. One of the most interesting is that she haunts the Harecastle tunnel at Kidsgrove and that if you walk through the tunnel you will hear the sound of her crying. Other people have caught sight of a female spectre without a head. The story goes that her husband had cut the poor girl's head from her body after discovering she had had a liaison with another man. There are also reports of this lady sitting on a boat jetty at Bathpool with her severed head in her lap, accompanied by the sound of loud weeping.

The Highwayman William Howe, Kinver

This is a ghost tale that has always fascinated me, for there are some associations to my own family in the story. William Howe was an unusual highwayman in that many of his robberies took place on foot, and he always carried exceptionally long pistols capable of killing a victim at some distance. The Kinver story concerns the murder of one local farmer, Benjamin Robbins of Dunsley Hall, who was known to my family in Kinver and was wickedly slain by William Howe (close to where the old Stewponey Hotel stands) in the early hours of 18 December 1812 as Benjamin made his way home in a very nasty snow storm. I also have family who lived in nearby Enville, Bridgnorth and Highley, and Howe became something of a terror to those in and around the dark country lanes that linked them.

Although it is suggested William Howe had family in Stourbridge, he also had links to London, where he went to hide out after poor Benjamin's murder, but this was to be his last crime, for not long afterwards he was captured, hung by the neck until dead and his body returned to Kinver for gibbeting. This meant that he would be placed in a large metal cage, hung from a strong tree and left there until his remains rotted and only his skeleton remained. As William Howe had his share of friends from the rogue community, it is claimed they eventually removed his skeleton and buried him in nearby Gibbet Wood. This is probably true, for there are reports that the skeleton of a small but powerful man was indeed dug up some years after his death in this area.

An artist's impression of the Kinver highwayman.

To this day, people say they have seen what they believe to be the ghost of William Howe. Among the reports are some very good accounts of incidents from farm folk, policemen, and also visitors to the area, who have all described seeing a small, powerful-looking man walking or running along lanes in a tricorn hat – often with pistols drawn in both hands. Many years ago, a good reporter friend of mine was stopped on a journey to Bridgnorth by a vision matching that description that vanished before his eyes. Other people claim to have heard the sound of a chain swinging from a tree, usually accompanied by the awful stench of rotting flesh. This is a most interesting case for any ghost hunter to investigate.

The entrance to Drakelow Tunnels. (Courtesy of Karen Westwood)

Drakelow Tunnels, Kinver

Here you will find a most amazing and vast collection of tunnels that run under parts of Kinver, Kidderminster and other parts of Staffordshire. They were apparently built as an underground hideout should Britain suffer a nuclear attack. This was a particular concern in the 1930s when another world war again became a highly likely possibility. by 1941, the construction of the tunnels was well underway and consisted of over four and a half miles of interconnecting tunnels. Several people were killed during their construction. In one incident, three men were crushed to death in a roof fall, while others were struck and killed by trucks that ran through the tunnels. Some

say that if you look closely enough, you can see the initials of those who gave their lives to create the tunnels in the sandstone walls close to where they died.

When investigating these tunnels with Team Prism, a local and highly respected team of paranormal investigators, one particular evening, I picked up the name Eckard Schmit some Russian people and was also guided to a wall that had Russian writing on it which said 'DO NOT ENTER'. During the evening I also sensed and saw many spectres that moved in and out of the darkness that I feel were relevant to the accidents that had been reported. There is many an interesting story still to come out of these tunnels, certainly of a historic nature and of a paranormal one too.

Philip Solomon and 'Team Prism' on a ghost hunt.

Old Joe was a regular visitor to the Compa, in Kinver.

Kinver

A short distance from the village of Kinver is an area known as the Compa. A very interesting story made national news some years ago when a local couple from the area called Reg and Jean used to receive a visitation from a ghost, or a spirit, known as old Joe, who had been a former land worker whilst alive. The couple were not at all nervous of Joe and were so aware of his presence that they actually set a place at the dinner table for him!

Kinver

Albert Jones told me of a very interesting experience he had some years ago. He was driving his lorry towards Shatterford when, in his mirror, he saw a motorcyclist coming up fast on his right-hand side. Being a narrow road, Albert pulled his lorry into the left-hand side to let the motorbike past. As it did so, Albert noticed it was a big red and chrome BSA Twin, a motorcycle which a few years previously had been very popular and had a most distinctive sound to its engine that could not be mistaken for a modern machine.

The powerful bike passed him and, apart from its make, the other thing that caught Albert's eye was a long white scarf that trailed behind the rider's jacket. Albert was not sure if the rider was wearing a helmet or not, and, as a bend was coming up, he returned his attention to the road. Just at that moment, he heard a very loud bang

A BSA motorbike, like the ghostly machine seen at Kinver.

and presumed a serious accident had happened round the bend. He stopped and climbed out of his vehicle, but, to his astonishment, absolutely nothing was to be seen.

Could this have been a ghostly re-enactment of a motorcycle accident many years ago, or is there another explanation? Locals tell me they are not aware of such an incident happening, in recent years at least, but perhaps with a little more investigation an answer to the mystery may be found.

Leek

The Mermaid Inn near Leek has a very strange story of a mermaid who lives in the waters of a nearby pool and calls people to come into the water. Legend has it that a young man once drowned in the dark waters, though research failed to substantiate this claim. Other people claim to have seen spectral dogs jumping into the water, apparently chasing after something not visible to the human eye. A bit of a *fishy* story, some might say!

The Swan, Leek

The Swan has been claimed as Leek's oldest house and dates back to 1620. The beautiful black and white building was said to be one of the locations for J.R.R. Tolkien's writings, the famous author of *The Hobbit* and *The Lord of The Rings*, and some have even claimed a visitation from the old literary master occurs on occasions, but there has certainly been much other paranormal activity here.

Barmaids often complain to the landlord of being the victim of a naughty and playful ghost that may pinch them or blow in their hair. One particular lady reported a rather more serious incident involving a bottle that flew through the air and hit her on the head, causing a large lump. Strangely, no bottle could be found, and it is doubtful that it had been thrown by anyone else, as the pub had not yet been opened to the public that day.

People who have visited or stayed at the Swan have also reported that when going into a room the door would close behind them on its own and, perhaps even more scary, on occasions would appear to be locked fast and yet would open quite easily when staff came to the rescue!

The White Horse of Leek

The north Staffordshire moors are vast and have many a tale of ghosts and spooks. The most famous and widely reported is the story of the headless horseman and his white horse. Legend has it that while living he had been a great warrior and had fought in a famous battle between the English and the Scots. He slew many Scotsmen before his own head was slashed from his body by the broadsword of a Scottish clansman. However, his well-trained horse charged on through the enemy, scaring and scattering many before galloping home to his Staffordshire residence with the headless body still in the saddle.

Since that day, many strange stories have been recorded. One farmer, a little worse for drink, claimed the headless rider rode up beside him, pulled him onto the back of his horse and led him on a most fearsome route over rough land, hedges and water. Legend has it the poor farmer was not at all grateful for his nightmare journey and died a few days later from his injuries and fright! Other people have reported seeing the headless rider on the moors in the company of a large black dog, and that he has acknowledged some folk by pointing his staff at them. Some believe this is a sign of imminent death for the unfortunate acknowledged person. Although this is an old story, in more recent years modern road users have also reported seeing such a figure, usually not far from Longnor or travelling towards Leek. The moors can be quiet and lonely at the best of times, but perhaps the company of the headless horseman would not be your first choice of travelling companion.

5

Paranormal Phenomena in Lichfield and Further Afield

BENEATH the streets of Lichfield, a young girl got lost and died in subterranean tunnels many years ago. Since then, several shops in the town have reported a number of strange experiences – an overwhelming majority claim they have witnessed the ghost of a little girl. One man said that his dogs would not enter the cellar of his building, and there has long been a rumour that suggests an old, blocked-up tunnel leads from his building to Lichfield Cathedral. Other shop keepers have reported that, while serving customers, they have caught sight of a young girl standing in the corner; a thin, little lass with dirty hands and face and long red hair, always with a very sad expression on her face.

One cleaning lady often sensed the presence of the poor young lass and felt that she was picking up the name Elspeth whenever she seemed to be near the entity. Research has not revealed a burial location for a child of that name – is poor Elspeth's body lying deep in the underground tunnels of Lichfield to this very day?

Lichfield

At one time the Walsall and Wolves manager, Colin Lee, lived at Hanch Hall with his wife Linda. This is a lovely historic building that had once been the home of the Orme family, stretching right back to the days of Elizabeth I. Colin did a lot of building work there himself and also oversaw some workmen.

I became quite good friends with Colin during his time at Wolverhampton Wanderers, and although the family had to sell the property because of his commitment to a very big job in football, he told me some interesting stories about Hanch Hall. Many strange things have been said to occur, including tools being moved about with no apparent reason, strange noises heard and mysterious fragrances permeating the air.

The building also has its own female ghost known as the Blue Lady. No one seems to know for sure who she is, but one woman who had visited the tea room, told me she had seen such a vision from the corner of her eye and described her as being quite small, immaculately dressed and with a lovely smell of lavender about her. Could she possibly be one of the ladies of the Orme family?

People speak of hearing the sound of dogs barking or running in and around the area, but rarely is anything seen. The sound of a hunting horn has also been heard in the nearby lanes. At one time, Longton had two mills, one water-driven and run by the Hunt family and one wind-driven. Both mills were eventually converted into private houses and in this area there have been reports of the sound of a ghostly hunting horn.

The King's Head, Lichfield

The King's Head in St John's Street has long been associated with the ghost of a Laughing Cavalier. A skirmish between Roundheads and Royalists during the Civil War took place outside the building and a story was told to me that the body of a Cavalier who had been murdered was secreted in the cellars. According to locals, he still moves in and around the building and particularly stands on the pavement. He has also been known to raise a pewter mug and take what appears to be a drink of ale.

One of the landlords, Sid Farmer, claims the building was linked to a young woman who had been burned to death there (or nearby) around 300 years ago and that she still makes a return visit to the site and that her name may have been Margaret or Margarite. More recently, a little girl walking in King Street asked her mother who the lady was in the awful raggedy clothes

and why did she smell wood burning. It seems to be one of those areas that seem to have regular occurrences of haunted happenings.

Lichfield

The cathedral is said to be haunted by some ghostly characters, yet when you make enquiries of the clergy there, they shake their heads and suggest it may be more to do with people's imaginations.

Generally, and not surprisingly, people have described seeing figures of a religious type both inside and around the outside of the cathedral itself, and several people have claimed that while in the cathedral they have heard someone sitting by them who was praying, but when they have looked have been surprised to see no one there. Almost everyone who has had a ghostly encounter at the cathedral has said they have been quite pleasant.

The Laughing Cavalier outside the King's Head.

Little Hay

Close to Lichfield, there is a place where a most unusual occurrence was experienced by a highly respected policeman some years ago. He would often do a bit of plastering in civic life, and, being a man of a kindly nature, had volunteered to help the owners of a little cottage in the village to restore it. However, it seems perhaps a former owner was not so pleased to see the policeman in the building helping with alterations, because every time he poured water into a bucket ready to mix the plaster, it all simply vanished before his eyes! Other people witnessed this happening too and the owners decided the cottage must surely be haunted and psychic mediums were asked to visit but with little success, and the plaster continued to vanish! Ultimately, a clergyman was asked to visit the cottage who came and simply prayed and it appears the ghost was finally appeased and quietened. From that day on no more difficulties were faced, that is except for the occasional beautiful fragrance of lavender, which the owners had no problem with at all.

Little Haywood

Here can be found Weetman's Bridge and the ghost of a young lady, who appears stressed and crying. Many people believe that she is the lady that legend says jumped to her death when facing great difficulties in her life. Whether the name Weetman has anything to do with her family name no one knows, but many claim that to this day she continues to weep.

Loggerheads

On the old B5026 road that leads to Eccleshall and on towards Newcastle under Lyme lies the village of Broughton, and the pretty church of St Peter. Directly opposite stands Broughton Hall – a great house with a most interesting history that also has its share of spooks. One spectral visitor is known by the name of Red Socks. A cleaning lady, whilst attending to her duties in the long gallery attic and staircase, felt that someone was standing by her. Turning and looking up, she saw what she described as a young man walking down the stairs in quite solid form. Rising up from her knees to stand back and show respect, she had the shock of her life as the figure walked straight through her physical body. One thing struck her greatly, and that was his red socks.

At Charnes Hall, the story is told of the ghost of a young woman looking for the wedding ring that was taken from her finger by a female servant after she had been laid out in her coffin. Numerous people have reported seeing a beautiful young woman in a billowing silk gown searching for that little band of gold. Other people claim, however, that the young lady who lay in the coffin was not actually dead, and was rather in a comatose state, and that it was actually a man who had chopped off her finger to steal the valuable ring.

The shock of the injury is believed to have brought the young wife back to consciousness. It is said that she actually recovered from her terrible ordeal and lived for many years before being buried with her husband in the churchyard at Eccleshall. Whatever the cause of this haunting is, it is a most fascinating story indeed.

The Dunrobin, Longton

This public house was once a very popular hotel, but has since been demolished to make way for housing. However, as many stories throughout this book have proved, the removal of a building does not necessitate the end of a ghost visitation or haunting. It was not unusual for shades in Victorian dress to be seen and it seems that one ghost in particular has continued to walk the area to this day, generally only seen by young people. The spectre is said to be clad in Victorian dress, black from head to toe, and carrying a bunch of keys that she rattles on a metal ring. Not everyone sees her; some just hear the jingling sound of her keys.

The Bingo Hall, Longton

The Bingo Hall used to be a cinema up until the 1970s, when it suffered the same fat as many other cinemas at that time and, sadly, closed. When the building was being used as a cinema, the former caretaker reportedly saw a ghostly figure in dark clothes drift across the balcony. Showing great courage, he challenged whatever it was that had appeared before him. On another occasion, the caretaker saw the same ghost again but, this time, he had his guard dog with him. This proved to be of little help, however, as the dog was most distressed. As the caretaker and his dog looked on, they saw the figure bend over the rails and then simply disappear completely. The dog shied away and refused to move forward; his hackles standing on end, and growling fiercely as it backed away from the vision.

Longton Hall

Longton Hall, which was knocked down in 1934, was considered by many to be a haunted building. Many people in the past describe seeing the prettiest girl you could imagine dressed all in white. Local people believe she had worked at the hall as a servant and caught the eye of a not-so-honourable gentleman, who, getting the poor lass in the family way, wasn't interested in the responsibility that would follow.

People believe she may have lived at a nearby farmhouse (which still stands to this day) and worked at the great hall on a daily basis. Certain information suggests that, rather than face the shame of being pregnant and unmarried, she committed suicide by drowning herself in one of the pools in the grounds. Many people today describe seeing a vision of her, even walking across roads where motorists have felt quite sure they have hit her, yet, when they stop to see if she is okay, there is no one in sight.

Another story relating to the hall is that one of its owners murdered his wife after discovering her indiscretions with one of the servants and that, on a New Year's Eve, which was when the crime took place, it was not unusual to see a lady dressed in a cloak and hat floating around the building. Some people describe seeing this similar vision in about 2006. Of course one must remember that you can remove a building but not a ghost, which may return to the site of their earthly life, usually quite unaware that anything has changed.

Middleton Hall

You can visit the still beautiful hall once lived in by Sir Hugh Willoughby, the great Tudor explorer, and Cassandra, the first duchess of Chandos. The house also has royal links to Queen Elizabeth I, Lady Jane Grey and the great authoress, Jane Austen. No wonder then that the present staff speak of seeing more than one beautiful and elegant lady that walks the building. Perhaps a rather stranger spectre is that of a gentleman dressed in a Civil War uniform with long hair. He has very effeminate mannerisms and could well be one of the original owners, perhaps with a history of dressing a little outlandishly. Many things go bump in the night, strange fragrances abode and even the sound of children's laughter has been known to ring out at Middleton Hall. This is a place I have investigated for several major ghost hunt companies and can certainly endorse as a most haunted building.

A Ghoulish Cyclist in Milford

A number of visitors have said that, when driving through this area, they have come upon a man riding an old-fashioned bicycle in what appears to be quite old-fashioned clothes for today. Perhaps not that unusual, but what is strange is that as they overtake this cyclist, he literally just vanishes from sight. Some people have said the vision appeared so quickly in front of them, they feared that they may have knocked the man from his bike. But you may have guessed from the context of this book that of course nothing can be seen when they have got out of their vehicle to check.

Some of the locals have put forward an answer to this man and his bike ride. Apparently, many years ago, a man had been killed at the bottom of a bore-shaft, at a pumping station which was quite close to Weetman's Bridge. Try as they might, rescuers had not been able to get him out and his final moments on earth were spent at the bottom of that shaft. Friends had spoken of the hard-working chap who always put in a good shift and always rode to work and home again on his bike. Perhaps the ethereal imprint from yesteryear of this man is of more pleasant moments than his sad demise. One can only hope that to be the case.

An Otherworldly Fairground in Milford Common

An unusual haunting which has been widely communicated is the sound of an old-fashioned fairground, when nothing is

Could the fair at Milford Common have looked something like this?

to be seen of such an event. Some of the locals claim this experience occurs particularly when it is windy. People say they can hear squeals of laughter, screams and chattering, and it can be quite disconcerting at times.

North Staffordshire Hospital

The newly built hospital stands on the site of what was formerly St Loy Hospital, which research suggests may well have been a leper hospital. Many of those in the medical profession will tell you that where such care has been offered in the past, hauntings seem to occur. Nurses at this hospital have often spoken of taking a break in a private room set aside for them. When alone, they have frequently claimed to feel the presence of someone in there with them.

In addition, they believe they have seen an elderly lady through the glass door in an old-fashioned hospital nightgown looking directly at them.

At one time, the building was also a workhouse and both staff and visitors have reported seeing ghostly children in a very poor state of dress. One nurse, who has mediumistic ability, felt the children were searching for their parents and this would not be at all unusual; in the workhouse, children were separated from their mothers and fathers and if they were particularly upset this could certainly be the trigger for this particular haunting. Other strange events include the sounds of whistling and singing. These are just a few of the unexplained occurrences that happen at this hospital and almost all hospitals around the UK report similar experiences of hauntings and the like.

Norton

Mick told me a very interesting story about a ghost known as the 'Owl Man'. Legend has it he was pecked to death by the owls that he used to feed with rats and mice. When his body was found in the old churchyard, rats had severely bitten his body. From that time, people have reported seeing the ghost of a man with no eyes who turns his head from side to side and stands by a particular tree in the churchyard. This is an interesting story, but one cannot help but wonder if this is an urban myth. I can't really imagine owls attacking a human being and research fails to come up with positive proof that anyone was found in the churchyard in this awful state.

Norton Canes Church

At the front of Norton Canes Church there are a few gravestones, but one has no name or religious markings – solely a skull and crossbones. This is said to be where the ghost of a very tall man with an unusual hat has appeared to people. One correspondent says he saw a spectre with a sabre in his hand and that he looked him straight in the eyes; surely enough to make you freeze on the spot out of sheer fright!

Norton in Hales

At the site of the ruins of St Margaret's Chapel legends abounded that at one time there was a clergyman who became involved in Black Magic, and even sacrifices of a most awful nature. Legend has it that when local people found out what the evil father was doing a group of them fired the chapel with him locked in the crypt. As his burnt remains were never recovered, it is said that an evil spirit entity remains to this day in the centre of what is left of the building. People say neither dogs nor other animals like to be taken there and even the fiercest of them will back away from what seems to be nothing at all to the human eye.

Rochester

There is an old farmhouse in Rochester which the owners claim have some strange paranormal happenings, such as the sound of balls bouncing in the middle of the night. A little investigation by them suggested that a boy and girl had died in the house at one time and it is believed it is the sound of the two of them playing that people hear to this day.

Rugeley

A very interesting story from 1782 concerns a young nurse called Eliza Hodgkinson, who had been given the charge of looking after a seven-year-old boy who was terminally ill. Nurse Eliza was asked to collect the boy from Rugeley Grammar School and, in the company of a servant, took him to his home and made the lad as comfortable as possible, before sitting up during the night beside him. But something strange had happened on the trip there. By a canal bridge very close to Rugeley Church, a lady walked up to them and asked if the rector was at home, who just happened to be the father of the poorly child.

'I must see him,' she explained.

Eliza replied, 'He is home, my dear, but you will not be able to see him tonight as there are great worries for the family at the moment.'

The woman insisted. 'I must see him, I have a child that must be buried this evening,' and pointed to an object wrapped in cloth under her cloak. The woman then just disappeared before their eyes.

Obviously, Eliza and the servant accompanying her were extremely concerned and spent as long as they could searching for her, but to no avail – she was gone. Eliza tended to her patient throughout the night. Unfortunately, in the early hours, the poor lad passed away. Nurse Hodgkinson kept the story of the woman to herself. However, the man servant had told others of the strange encounter they both had on their way. Eventually, in a solicitor's letter, Eliza told the story, which was to be told only to those with an appropriate interest, but as the years have rolled by the story has become more public and it would seem that the woman the good nurse had seen had come to warn her that a young person would die very shortly. It seems that person was her young patient.

Hoo Mill Locks, Rugeley

At Hoo Mill Locks, near Rugeley, people regularly report the sound of a woman screaming for help. Other people describe the vision of a woman on the other side of the canal who waves and seems to be trying to get their attention. This could be relevant to the canal boat murder of poor Christina

Collins on the Trent and Mersey Canal in 1839. Christina was actually a Nottingham-born girl, the daughter of an inventor of fishing nets.

By the time Christina's parents died in 1818, she had made a very good marriage to an older man, Thomas Ingle, a quite famous magician of his time, known as The Emperor, who toured theatres throughout the UK. His act was a gruesome one, which at times was probably more like a horror show, such as cutting off the head of a chicken before miraculously bringing it back to life, and other such ghoulish magic tricks.

Christina accompanied and joined in her husband's shows working as a singer and dancer and later became his assistant. They had no children and unfortunately Thomas died reasonably young, leaving his pretty widow of thirty years behind.

It wasn't long until she met Robert Collins, the love of her life, and they were married in 1838. She became a seamstress and Robert moved to London to find good work as a stable hand. He quickly found himself in the position of being able to send the money for his wife to join him in London. Times had been financially difficult for the couple and she could not afford to travel by stagecoach or the railway, and thus decided to take the much slower but cheaper form of travel by barge on the Trent and Mersey Canal. She paid sixteen shillings for her fare on a boat belonging to Pickford and Company and skippered by James Owen, along with two other men, George Thomas and William Ellis, and a boy assistant, Billy Musson.

During the journey, Christina came to realise she was in trouble. They were a rough and lecherous group who were making very rude remarks about what they would like to do to her of a sexual nature, and, on several occasions, she had tried to find a way of leaving the boat and reaching London another way. One evening, approaching midnight and travelling through Hoo Mill Locks, the lock keeper and his wife saw the pretty young woman standing on top of the cabin crying out for help and saying she would not go down into the cabin. Rushing from their home, the lock keeper's wife insisted on knowing what was going on. One of the men answered that he was the husband of the woman and quickly pushed her down into the cabin.

This was the last time Christina Collins was seen alive. Her corpse was found in the canal at Brindley Bank near Rugeley the next morning. The boatmen were duly charged with the rape and murder of Christina Collins and were sent to jail in Stafford, although Billy Musson was released without charge.

An appeal saved William Ellis from hanging, with evidence that he had showed less intent to the crime than his companions. Owen and Thomas, although escaping the crime of rape from lack of evidence, swung for the murder at Stafford jail on 11 April 1840, where 10,000 people had flocked to witness their demise. The hangman had perhaps not prepared the noose properly and it is alleged his assistant was required to hang onto the legs of the prisoners to break their necks as they jigged about on the end of the rope.

It is a terrible story, and one would hope this is only a psychic replay of the final moments of poor Christina's life and that what is sensed is just a ghostly image of yesteryear. Her spirit must surely be on the other side amongst her loved ones.

The Fishing Pool, Rugeley

Halfway between Rugeley and Cannock there is a particular fishing pool that has been the site of various strange apparitions. Peter Berry was there one evening intending to fish throughout the night. When he set out his stool, rods and other equipment, he suddenly saw standing behind him a man in what he described as very old-fashioned clothes, wearing a large broad-brimmed hat and carrying what looked like a heavy stick or stave, which he proceeded to bang several times on the ground. Peter felt this was clearly to gain his attention but, strangely, as he went to speak to the figure, it vanished before his eyes.

Other people who fished this pool have also described the sound of banging but far less have actually seen the ghost. The ghost is known locally as Sir Reynolds, but who he is or where he comes from no one seems to know.

Rugeley

The library at Rugeley has had many reports of hauntings and ghosts. Cleaning staff have described catching sight of people from the corner of their eye, but when looking round, they could see that no one was there. Clearer visions have been seen of a lady dressed in Victorian-style clothes and a gentleman in a cap in the upstairs Reference Library. Downstairs, there have been stories of objects being moved and unexplainable voices beckoning people to a certain area. Some of the staff who worked

An artist's impression of the so-called Doctor Dark – the figure of many a child's nightmare.

there in the past preferred, if at all possible, not to work in the building on their own, especially when it was near to closing time or when no one was about.

The Shrewsbury Arms, Rugeley

I was informed by one of my correspondents that the Shrewsbury Arms was the regular haunt of Staffordshire's most famous poisoner, Dr Palmer. Although not in recent years, rather for a period of about five or six years some time ago, this spectre was regularly seen in the building or coming round a corner wearing a black cape, black hat and carrying a doctor's bag in one hand, and some strange-looking object in the other. It has been argued that the spectre is more likely to have been that of John Parsons-Cook, who had actually been one of Palmer's poison victims, and whose post-mortem took place at the Shrewsbury Arms.

Other locals suggest, however, that it may have been another doctor they call Old Vaughan, who is again seen in the nearby streets in the hours of darkness or in the twilight hours and has been nicknamed 'Doctor Dark' by youngsters, who were warned if they were naughty, Doctor Dark would come for them.

A Creepy Cottage in Shallowford

Shallowford is home to the former sixteenth-century cottage of Isaac Walton, who once lived quite near to Stone. Isaac Walton was of course the famous author of the *Complete Angler* and some people claim to have seen a ghost or spirit that may be the great fisherman himself. But better known is the ghost of a lady called Miriam, who people describe as being very dark with thick, greasy hair and rather dour in manner.

Strange things have often happened in the cottage, including lights that switch on and off by themselves and electric equipment that starts up for no apparent reason. In and around the area of Walton's cottage, people have reported seeing a man wearing the type of clothes popular in the seventeenth century who walks through quite solid objects such as trees or hedges and on what appears to be an ancient pathway, before simply dissolving from view.

Shugborough Hall

Mary Jeavons told me of a strange experience she had one evening whilst leaving Shugborough Hall and its lovely estate.

The exit of Shugborough Estate.

The tower on Shugborough Estate, where a strange flashing light was seen.

As she and her three friends reached the end of the road that takes you out of the estate, two of the women saw quite clearly a young woman in a long, flowing white dress run across the road and into the fields to their right, whereas the other lady saw nothing at all. At this time it was getting quite late and darkness was starting to fall. The lady who had not seen the vision pointed out a light that kept flashing and seemed to be coming from the top of a tower-like building. They didn't think it was a camera-flash because, although it seemed to be going on and off, it stayed on for quite a while, at least ten to fifteen seconds. Making their way home and discussing their experiences they said the next time they visited the estate they would go back to where they had seen the vision of the girl and find out what the tower was. When they did go back some time later they felt rather disappointed as the tower appeared to be derelict and unoccupied. Could this ghost have been making her way towards the tower with the help of someone with a light on to show the way?

Originally, Sinai House was made up of two buildings and later turned into one. It is a Grade Two listed building and is made up of medieval, Jacobean and eighteenth-century structure. On first appearance it appears to be a typical Elizabethan manor house, but is in fact much older. Some historians and architects have described it as the most important house in England. Much of the building is in a poor and dangerous condition but is currently in the process of being restored to its former majesty.

Historical research suggests it may have stood on the site of a Roman stronghold and that, in medieval times, trials and courts may have been conducted at the building. Following the Dissolution of the Monasteries, the Paget family received it into their ownership. It was also an important site during the Civil War where several minor battles were fought near to Sinai House. Lord Henry Paget is alleged to have had his leg shot off whilst riding a horse at the side of Wellington at the Battle of Waterloo. Wellington is reported to have said quite calmly, 'I do believe you have lost a leg Sir Henry,' who replied, equally calmly, 'Sir, I do believe I have.'

Sir Henry was well-known as a ladies' man and is said to have cast his eye upon many women around the area and was eventually involved in a high profile divorce case, which lost him his wife and a considerable amount of his riches! The Pagets owned the house and lands up until the 1900s, when it was turned into a collection of cottages, which eventually were turned into pig sties and hen runs! People have always spoken of the ghosts of Sinai and the spirits and spectres that travel from one room to another. The owner's cat would sit yowling with its eyes fixed on something no one else could see.

The house of course had its own Grey Lady and an unusual legend suggests that she had been a very good and moral young woman who had been seduced by a monk or monks from the local area and that when she had told them she was with child, they murdered her and buried her in a field nearby. From that day on, apparently she

walks across the bridge over the moat, particularly around Christmas and New Year time. Although the current owners have not seen her personally, various psychics and mediums have picked up on her presence.

Other people have reported a hay cart that passes by and vanishes from sight and the sound of what they believe are Cavaliers and Roundheads fighting. Some poltergeist activity has also been reported and crockery and other utensils fly around the kitchen, and the owner himself has allegedly seen the famous Black Dog of Sinai in the dining room and kitchen. These huge black dogs were again claimed to be associated to the monks or even to have belonged to the abbot himself. Certainly this seems to be a most paranormally active place with a considerable amount of ghosts and hauntings taking place.

6

Spooky Events in and around Stafford

THERE is a very interesting story from one of the Rising Brook Writers' books called *Tales of the Supernatural*, about the Ancient High House in Stafford. This is a building that has stood for over 400 years and has been a Civil War officers' prison, a school, a grocer's store and today is a museum. In 2006, the *Most Haunted* team visited the building and had some quite remarkable experiences; heavy oak doors on the top floor were seen to open and close independently, and the team also witnessed a tall, spectral figure in a doorway on the top floor.

The third floor has certainly had its share of ghostly sightings in the past, including an elderly lady who sits in a rocking chair in the so-called Victorian Room, the vision of a pretty young girl who stands staring blankly ahead in the centre of that same room, and several cold spots. There is also a very old well in the back yard – legend suggests this was the burial site of a young child. Perhaps it is no wonder that reports come through of a naughty child ghost who locks women in the ladies' toilets and moves objects to different places. People

also speak of Mrs Marston's ghost, a lady from the early 1900s, who so loved the building that some claim she has never left and hers may well be the smiling face that is seen in and around the building.

Perhaps a most amazing story, again from the Rising Brook Writers' book, recalls that, in the 1960s, a group of American tourists were taken on a tour of the Ancient High House by the grocer from next door and thoroughly enjoyed themselves, if a little startled by the accuracy of his commentary. They were even more startled the next day when they returned and were told their tour guide had actually died fifty years previously. Apparently, this story made national news in one of the tabloid newspapers.

Over the years, the Ancient High House has changed a great deal and for many years it was actually two houses that linked together on the upper levels and was attached to Shaw House and the Swan Hotel. The so-called 'grand lady' who walks the upper corridors has been witnessed in all three buildings but seems to particularly favour Shaw House. Locally, people also speak of Naughty

Mary, a remarkably pretty girl with bright red hair who is known to touch people and pull their hair, especially if you share her shade of colour.

Other spirits include a woman who is said to either be dressing or undressing herself in an upper storey front room. She has also been seen leading a gentleman into the room – where there is a four-poster bed. One can only imagine what for!

There is also a vision of a woman who walks through the walls of the ladies' toilets and many say they still smell the quite distinctive aroma of someone smoking a pipe, whereas on other occasions there is strong smell of roses or lavender. This is a place where anyone interested in the paranormal will certainly be pleased to visit.

It is a museum now and can be visited for free. Now that sounds like a 'spooktacular' bargain to me!

The Broad Eye Windmill

Joy told me of an interesting experience she had while driving round the island that stands in front of the Broad Eye Windmill in Stafford. In the very early hours of the morning she felt quite sure she saw a tall man in a top hat and black clothes holding the hand of what appeared to be a very small woman or child and scurrying across the road towards the Broad Eye Windmill. Joy decided to turn back to see what it was she had witnessed but could see nothing at

Broad Eye Windmill.

all. Could the man and small person have had something to do with one of the buildings in this area? It certainly was an odd experience and it would be interesting to know if anyone else has seen this unusual couple.

Church Lane

In Church Lane there is a sixteenth-century eating house in the old quarter of the town and it is here you may be told the story of Ethel, who, if she likes you, is most welcoming, but if you are not to her taste, you may see plates and cutlery fly off the shelves. Former staff referred to her as the 'soup kitchen ghost'.

Eccleshall Castle, Stafford

Eccleshall Castle has a very strange atmosphere at times and one story was told to me by Doreen Greson, a most down-to-earth lady, of strange happenings revolving around the legend of a White Lady, a Grey Lady and a Cavalier. Also, an unusually huge black dog is sometimes seen at dusk, but that no one considers it to be a bad omen in any way and, in fact, its sighting is much more likely to warn you of danger.

Another woman claimed that once, while walking round the castle site, she felt someone following her and was quite unnerved, but also felt the protection of her old Labrador, Bess, who had died some years previously. Could this have instead been the large ghost dog that was protecting her?

Someone else told me that the Grey Lady would sometimes be seen with what looked like a stone wall behind her and wearing what could have been bridal wear and being very beautiful yet sad-looking. This would be an ideal site for investigation.

The Super Bowl

The Super Bowl is a modern building, but many people have suggested that in the ancient past the land belonged to an old infirmary that was also used as the town's morgue. One man who worked at the bowling alley said that sometimes, when you were working on the bowling lanes, you could clearly hear the sound of mumbling and at other times you would feel that people were following you. A cleaner who worked there at one time said she saw the horrific vision of a hanging man in the Quasar area.

The Old Gaol

Outside the walls of the old gaol was historically the scene of public hangings. Huge crowds of many thousands would make their way from all parts of the country to witness the final moments of some poor soul's final demise. Research suggests that many of these villains were not convicted of murder, rape or other terrible crimes, but such crimes as horse stealing or robbery, which could result in them swinging by the neck until they were dead. In 1856, we are told that almost 30,000 people jammed the front of the gaol to watch the execution of notorious Rugeley poisoner, Dr William Palmer.

It was in 1914 when the final execution took place here and is little wonder today that people claim to hear the sounds of screams, the thud of the hangman's drop, and the vision of men, women and even children wringing their hands in terror. One respected person also claimed she had seen what she believed to be the ghost of Dr Palmer himself with his little black bag in hand right outside the building.

The Gatehouse Theatre

The Gatehouse Theatre, like every theatre in the UK, has its reports of ghosts. Perhaps the most famous one is the lady who walks down the main stairs of the theatre in beautiful clothes and is often referred to by the cleaning staff as 'the posh lady'. Some people also refer to her as the Grey Lady.

Other reports are of the fragrance of lavender, roses and sudden bumps and bangs that have no accountable source. Strangely enough, the Gatehouse Theatre rarely has psychics or mediums appear on it's show lists, which is perhaps a little unfortunate as they may be able to put a name to the lady on the stairs. Staff also speak of a little boy who is believed to have been a stable boy, and is usually seen around the back of the building.

Shire Hall Library

The library in Shire Hall is where a spectre known as Claude is said to walk through walls that join the Shire gallery, even making his way down to the Tourist Information Centre on occasions.

But where does Claude come from? I ask this because, in my investigations of other areas, there is certainly a man called Claude who catches the trains in and out of Wolverhampton, but has also been seen at Derby and Crewe stations as well, carrying his top hat and silver cane. Could it be that his spirit also travels to the Shire Hall in Stafford?

Wetherspoons

At one time, the Wetherspoons building in Stafford had been a cinema. Staff say that during quiet moments, after the building has closed, the sound of a projector is often heard rolling and clicking away from the old projection room, yet when checked out nothing is to be seen. Glasses get moved around the building without human hands, footsteps, voices that whisper and the sound of two people crossing the balcony are also heard. On one occasion, a member of staff claimed to have seen the couple stumbling arm-in-arm as if they had perhaps been sampling some of the spirits from this world!

The Surgery

In the town you will find a popular bar known as The Surgery, although at one time it was better known by locals as the Noah's Ark. Music often rings out from this popular bar, but people report hearing the sound of people singing songs of yesteryear when the pub is actually closed. Staff say that when the bar is empty fur-

Spooky phone calls.

niture gets re-arranged and there are parts of the building that have terribly cold areas despite efforts being made to warm that part. Mobile phones have also been known to ring but register as being a non-existent call. Other people describe being pushed or pinched and some ladies have enquired of staff who it is crying in the ladies' toilets, but on investigation there is never anyone there. One correspondent told me, 'Without a shadow of a doubt, Philip, there is a man, lady and some sort of animal that haunts that building and it can be quite scary at times.'

The Alexandra Hotel

The modern day Superdrug store stands on the site of what was at one time the Alexandra Hotel, a spooky looking house covered in creeping ivy that was knocked down in the 1960s to build a Tesco store. Legend has it that at times, particularly in the store room area, people feel someone standing behind them and, if they are female, touch them or blow in their hair. Other people have spoken of seeing an elegantly dressed man with a cane in hand who stands outside the shop and has even been known to doff his hat before vanishing into thin air. This is clearly a spirit rather than a ghost, because he actually interacts with people, and perhaps he is returning to what he still considers to be a hotel rather than a pharmacy.

Stafford Castle

The castle has a headless horseman who rides around the castle's lands. This sighting was reported many years ago, but in more recent times, during the 1960s, was witnessed by a caretaker who, although sceptical of such things, felt quite sure he had seen the spectre riding by. Doors also open and slam shut for no apparent reason and people will say, 'That's Admiral Anson barging through the building once again!' Another strange occurrence is the sound of a clock ticking very loudly in a room that doesn't contain a clock which makes such a loud and distinctive sound.

My wife, Kath, had a very odd experience one Sunday afternoon recently when visiting Stafford Castle. Quite a steep hill leads up from the gates to the castle itself and the council provide toilet facilities at the bottom of the hill. Going into the ladies' toilets, she says there was no one else in there, yet, strangely, she felt there was another lady present. Just as she went through the doorway, the hand drier started up, but absolutely no one else was in there.

When Kath came out of the cubicle, she washed her hands and used the drier to dry them. She then decided to see just what had caused the drier to start up of its own accord, suspecting it must have been the movement from her that had done it. So, stepping back, she walked past it expecting it to start up, but it didn't! She then went outside the building and decided to walk back in again, to check if it was her movement that had caused it, but once again the drier was completely silent. She felt quite sure there was some paranormal force causing the equipment to work of its own accord. I'm not really surprised by this report as toilets often seem to be haunted places, but for what reason I really cannot begin to explain.

Mysterious Staffordshire

Doug Pickford tells a few fascinating Staffordshire ghost stories in his excellent book, *Staffordshire: It's Magic and Mystery.* One in particular involved his own father. Apparently, his father drove a travelling shop van for a company from Rudyard during the 1950s. These types of vans and travelling salesmen were quite common at the time and he often visited the farms and houses of the remote Staffordshire moorlands, becoming friends with some of the farming folk who would be waiting for him with tea, biscuits and perhaps a little chat, and it wasn't unusual for his father to offer people a lift from farm to farm. One day, as he drove past Royal Cottage in Cornford during a terrible winter snowstorm and with dusk drawing in, he noticed an elderly lady making her way along the road in some difficulty due to the conditions. In true gentlemanly fashion, he stopped the vehicle and asked the lady if she would like a lift. She immediately replied that she would and started to make her way to the rear of his van and round to the passenger side. He waited for some minutes, but the elderly woman did

*Stafford Castle: home to
a headless horseman?*

Stafford Castle.

not arrive at the passenger door. Fearful that she had slipped in the snow, he left the vehicle to search for her, but nothing was to be found except a collection of footprints that led from his door to just short of the passenger door. He searched as best he could, but nothing was to be seen of the old lady, who he never saw again.

The Victoria Hotel, Stoke-on-Trent

The Victoria Hotel in Fletcher Road has an unusual ghost story – related to me by a lady who worked there at one time – of a painter and decorator who had passed away whilst working inside the building. At the end of the day, he would always have a couple of pints of beer before banging the empty glass down on the bar and saying goodbye, but the strange thing is that after his passing, numerous bar staff reported the sound of a glass being banged down on the bar, but when turning round no one was to be seen.

Church Road, Stoke-on-Trent

Sarah contacted me to tell me about her family's experiences in her childhood home in Church Road, Stoke-on-Trent, about thirty years ago. The house, which had been built in 1823, was in very close proximity to St Bartholomew's Church and two graveyards, where the people who once lived in the house are buried.

Various things were experienced including hearing footsteps and smelling a smoky, gunpowder smell, and also the smell of a pipe. There were numerous occasions when her parents could hear footsteps in their bedroom, only to discover that Sarah and her brother were fast asleep in their own rooms. On one of these occasions, after her father had been upstairs to investigate the noise, he came back down and could see a brush, which was hanging on the hall stand, swinging back and forth. Sarah, who describes her father as probably the most straight-laced person you could meet, says he was in his bedroom one day with his foot up on a chest tying his shoe laces, when he felt something physically push past him which, understandably, quite unnerved him. On one occasion, as her brother was going into his bedroom, he saw a hand resting on his snooker table, which quickly disappeared as he entered the room.

Sarah says that as young children, they were too scared at night to go to the bathroom, which was downstairs and at the other side of the house, so they had a portable loo upstairs. Sarah's bedroom was situated at the top of the stairs and she always feared that whatever came upstairs would get her first! However, one evening she braved going downstairs on her own, but as she passed the window (the street light was on outside), she expected her shadow to appear in the square of light that was thrown onto the wall. Instead, the square of light disappeared, as though something was totally blocking the window. As the light was still on outside, this really spooked her and she didn't dare to go any further.

Sarah's mother said that when she was about six, she had shouted that she could see a man on the stairs and that she could see through him. Her grandfather said that she had described this man exactly as a 'Peeler' (an old-time policeman), and someone she would not have come across as they were well before her time. Sarah says her mother often thought she could see someone passing across the bottom of the stairs, out of the corner of her eye. When they left the house about five years later, someone else moved in. Apparently he didn't stay there long – it seems that when he returned from work, he would find all his ornaments turned round the other way. Another family who lived there told Sarah their youngest child was too scared to sleep in her old bedroom and, after a while, started having trouble sleeping in her brother's old bedroom as well. It was recommended to them that they have the house exorcised. The person who performed the exorcism told them the house was built on what would have been linear lines in Pagan times, that Sarah's bedroom had two time zones, and that her brother's bedroom was the scene of a violent death. They also reported hearing the footsteps and smelling the smoky smell that Sarah and her family had experienced while they lived in the house. Sarah and her family have no doubt that the house was haunted. She says they never felt threatened by anything, she was just very scared while she lived there.

Tamworth Castle

I don't think it would be a shock to hear that Tamworth Castle has many ghosts with its history as the focal point of the kingdom of Mercia. With a castle that has stood proudly for over 1,000 years, one would be surprised if it wasn't haunted! I have to say I *know* it is.

The White Lady is said to walk the battlements and has been seen by so many people over the years that her ghost is almost impossible to reject. Legend has it the White Lady had been the lover of Sir Tarquin, a mighty knight of the realm. The castle would often hold jousting tournaments in the Lady Meadow Terrace below the castle. As she sat and watched such an event one day, her beloved was slain by Sir Lancelot, the famous knight of the King Arthur legends. Inconsolable, it said that since that time she makes a nightly return to the terrace and can be seen weeping for the death of her sweetheart.

Equally important to Tamworth is the Black Lady. In life, she is believed to have been a nun, who historians at the castle feel is the ghost of St Editha, who was cast out from her abbey at Polesworth by Roger Le Marmion, the all-powerful baron who, upon inheriting Tamworth from William the Conqueror very shortly after the Battle of Hastings, decided much would change. In 1139, the spirit of the Black Lady is said to have visited Marmion, pointed at him and claimed he was an evil and lecherous man. One can only wonder what this meant (or perhaps not if you have a vivid imagination). She also warned him that unless he restored her Benedictine abbey and its lands, he would suffer a terrible death. Legend has it she also hit him with her staff, causing a very bad wound to his head that would not heal.

Marmion had been extremely scared by his experience and decided to restore Polesworth Abbey and hand it back to its rightful owners and it is said his wound

Tamworth Castle.

then quickly healed. Or did it? For a few years later he died 'an unpleasant death'. If you wish to pay a visit to Tamworth Castle they have some fascinating electronic recreations, which I will not tell you about here as it would spoil a super experience, and you can visit the room the Black Lady haunts.

Over the years I have got to know quite a few of the staff who work at the castle and many report strange sounds and sudden drops in temperature.

Do visit the spiral staircase in the southwest turret in St Editha's Church. Many have had an unusual experience there and say as you walk up the steps you get the sense of someone walking past that is neither visible or of this world.

Tompkin

A tiny village not far from Endon, Tompkin still has its place in English history and haunted Staffordshire's legends too. During the time when Bonny Prince Charlie came this way, South Staffordshire was a place that provided rest and sustenance and if there was a great house or building nearby, the Scottish warriors would require feeding, watering and entertaining and to refuse such would probably result in a very quick death for owner or tenant alike!

One such group of Scotsmen took up part-time residence at the home of Squire Murhall who hated them but put on a pretence of some support to save him and his family difficulties. The Scotsmen went to bed in his home, cleared his table of food and drunk whatever was available. When they moved on, he waved them goodbye but Squire Murhall's fury rose. Gathering a few of his men, he noticed a little drummer boy limping after his Scottish comrades. Squire Murhall and his party cut him off and dragged him back to their home, where the boy was whipped mercilessly and skinned whilst still alive – the best part used to make a drum. Legend has it that for many years the drum could be seen at St Luke's Church in Endon, but so much bad luck seemed to come to the area, such as unusual deaths to farm livestock and suddenly ruined crops, that the clergy ordered it to be removed and buried.

Ever since that time people have reported seeing the little drummer boy and hearing the sound of drumming, Scottish voices, the drone of bagpipes and terribly child-like screams. Some people believe that the boy would have only been about thirteen and that his name was Tam. It would have been a terrible death and just the sort of crime to cause a haunting in my experience. Other people in this area claim to hear the sound of a man shouting for help and screaming. One can only wonder if the little boy's Scottish soldier friends have returned to pay back Squire Murhall.

Trentham

Trentham is an important area, historically speaking, for members of the family of King Wulfhere lived here at a place known as Trickingham, which may have been the original name for the area and over the years has developed into Trentham.

Trentham Hall and gardens is a wonderful place to visit and had an important convent here until Henry VIII's Dissolution of the Monasteries. James Leveson, who became the owner of this stately home in the 1500s, greatly developed the lands and, by marriage, the family became known as Leveson-Gower. Unfortunately, it is said that the family preferred London life and by avoiding Trentham, the hall and gardens eventually became very run-down and ultimately much of the house and other buildings had to be demolished.

Many ghosts are said to walk Trentham. The famous Grey Lady is seen walking in the Italian Garden. She is believed to have been a servant who may have risen to some standing within the family, either through marriage or another relationship.

Other visitors to the site have reported the sound of sweetly playing music that seems to come from no obvious source and of the shade of a man that walks with a hound on a leash, which he appears to release before both vanish from sight. Perhaps he was a gardener or gamekeeper who enjoyed catching the hares and rabbits that were common in the vicinity at that time, and probably still are if you know where to look for them!

Trentham Gardens is certainly a lovely, peaceful place to visit, but it seems it may have a degree of restlessness at times that attracts ghosts and spirits from the other side.

Tutbury Castle

This must surely be one of the most haunted buildings in the country, let

Tutbury Tower.

alone Staffordshire! The curator there is my good friend Lesley Smith, who is both an historian and famous for her appearances in the TV programme *Most Haunted*. I have also worked for paranormal organisations at the castle myself and can absolutely endorse it to genuinely having its fair share of ghosts, spooks and shades of yesteryear.

It is not at all surprising that the castle is so haunted, for it is an ancient historical site. Legend says the fort stood in Saxon times and was visited by Robin of Loxley, who eventually became better known as Robin of the Hood. After 1066, with William's conquering of England, Henry De Ferrers, one of his main supporters, was given Tutbury in recognition of his service.

Ghosts are often seen to this day, including a monk in a brown robe in a part of the castle known as the Vine Croft, where beer and ale was brewed. Another ghost is seen in the watchtower. Some people describe this lady as the White Lady, but it is my belief this is the ghost of Mary Queen of Scots, who was held at Tutbury Castle between 1569 and 1570 and 1585 to 1586. The story of the White Lady goes that she met her lover here, but in one meeting found him lying dead – put to the sword at the hands of her husband's men – and that she immediately threw herself to her death from the tower. Other legends have it that she impaled herself on the drawn sword of one of her husband's men, although some suggest it may have been the master himself that struck the killer blow.

One of the rooms at Tutbury Castle was slept in by Charles II, and people who have spent the night in this room claim to have seen a lady in grey. In another room, the spirit of a little girl called Lizzie visits and seems to enjoy playing and teasing those who set up paranormal investigations within!

It is at the gates of the castle where I had the strange experience of seeing a huge Norman knight, who bellowed at me and the group in my company, 'Be gone from here!' A little investigation seems to point to this knight being one of the Ferrer's family who, indeed, are buried in the ruins of the chapel of the castle. It is said that in Saxon times the chapel was known as St Michael's on the Hill, but renamed St Peter's on the instructions of the Normans, but why the ghost of the knight orders people from the castle no one knows.

Tutbury Castle.

The interior of Tutbury Castle.

If you visit this wonderful haunted building, Lesley Smith will tell you far more of its history of than I can, but it is certainly nice to include a place where I have had paranormal experiences myself. Former custodians of the castle all seem to conclude that the place is very haunted. Barry Valens was there for some time, as was Henry Ludlam, who from 1909 right through to 1950, during his charge, found the castle to be a most haunted place.

Tutbury Castle.

The interior of Tutbury Castle.
(Courtesy of Martyn Boyes)

Tutbury Castle by moonlight.
(Courtesy of Martyn Boyes)

There have been many reports of ghosts and ghouls at Weston Hall. In the past the building was used as a lunatic asylum and a rest building for those who were impoverished.

During the Second World War, many ATS girls were stationed in Stafford and were assigned beds in the great hall. I have been told on very good authority from family friends that most of these young ladies much preferred to sleep in tents in the grounds than inside the hall, where many reported hearing the sounds of terrible screams in the night, seeing the vision of the famous Grey Lady and other poor souls, who they described as being dressed in rags with hands held out before them. On opening the bar area in the morning, the staff would find it had been meticulously cleaned and polished when no cleaning staff had been on duty the previous night. When development took place a few years ago, several workers downed tools and refused to work on their own, instead insisting on working in pairs.

The Whittington Inn is a 700-year-old property with interesting historical links to royalty and perhaps London's most famous mayor, Dick Whittington. It also lays claim to having the spectre of Lady Jane Grey regularly visit from the other world. This apparition has valid foundations, for her family had exceedingly close links to Enville Hall in the local area.

The building is also haunted by less famous figures, including the ghost of Mary, who is said to repeatedly make herself known to men of a more handsome disposition! Dick Whittington himself visited and had close associations with this beautiful inn. Built in 1310 by Sir William De Whittington, knight and holder of most of the lands around Kinver, the knight is at times reported to be seen in full armour in fields nearby.

Legend has it that Sir William's grandson was the famous Richard (Dick) Whittington who went to London and became mayor of the city on three occasions. In truth, history would suggest it is more likely that he came from Gloucestershire, but a close association is not out of the question considering the surname.

During the Civil War in the 1640s, research suggests that King Charles hid in a priest hole at Whittington Manor following the battle of Worcester. Likewise, in 1711, Queen Anne spent a night at the manor house, which some people now actually claim is the site of Whittington's Hall Farm.

The Whittington Inn, said to be the regular haunting site for Lady Jane Grey.

were very pleased with them, but one picture was to stand out particularly. It showed the bride standing in front of a grave, with another face clearly showing on the gravestone. The family were quite certain that this was the bride's elder sister, who had died some years before, and they felt very honoured that she had come from the other side to be at her little sister's wedding. I believe our loved ones come to many such gatherings, but it is very rare indeed to have a picture of them in your family album!

It is also alleged that the Whittington Inn is where William Howe was apprehended following the murder of Benjamin Robbins, a distant relative of the author of this book, and people speak of his spirit appearing on occasions.

Undoubtedly, the Whittington Inn that stands on the A449 road to Kidderminster is a most haunted building.

Wombourne

A few years ago, I was allowed to take a copy of a fascinating and extremely unusual photograph to place in my collection of photos of ghosts and the paranormal. It is a picture of a couple who had been married at their local church and, as is often the case, the photographer had taken various pictures in and around the area, including the gravestones, some of which belonged to the relatives of the bride.

When the photographs were developed, the bride, groom and all the family

Yoxall

This is where the young apprentice of a local blacksmith is alleged to have committed suicide when he could stand the ill-treatment of his master no more. Following his death at his own hands (supposedly), the boy was buried without religious ceremony. Legend has it that years later, the skeleton of a young lad was found in nearby land with a spear through his remains. To this day, it has been claimed that sensitive animals, such as horses, fear to tread near the spot.

Bibliography

Books

Arnall, Carol, *Mysterious Happenings*, 2009,
  Davies

Bell, David, *Ghosts and Legends of
  Staffordshire and The Black Country*, 1994,
  Countryside Books

Bell, David, *Staffordshire and the Black
  Country Murder Casebook*, 1996,
  Countryside Books

Bell, David, *Staffordshire Tales of Mystery and
  Murder*, 2005, Countryside Books

Hunt, Anthony, *Murders Unsolved*, 2002,
  Quercus

Pickford, Doug, *Staffordshire: Its magic and
  Mystery*, 1994, Sigma Leisure

Pipe, Marian, *Secret Staffordshire: Ghosts,
  Legends and Strange Tales*, 1994, S.B.
  Publications

Poole, Charles Henry, *The Customs,
  Superstitions and Legends of the County of
  Stafford*, 1875, Roney & Co.

Rising Brook Writers, *Tales of The
  Supernatural*, 2007

Solomon, Philip, *Haunted Black Country*,
  2009, The History Press

Solomon, Philip, *Haunted Derby*, 2007,
  Tempus Publishing Ltd

Solomon, Philip, *Haunted Telford,* 2011, The
  History Press

Solomon, Philip, *Ghost Legends and Psychic
  Snippets*, 1990, PKN Publications

Solomon, Philip, *Ghosts of the Midlands
  & How to Detect Them*, 1990, PKN
  Publications

Solomon, Philip, *Ghosts & Phantoms of
  Central England*, 1997, PKN Publications

Newspapers & Websites

Wolverhampton Express & Star
Staffordshire Advertiser
Black Country Bugle
Evening Mail
BBC Radio Midlands
www.wikipedia.org

Other titles published by The History Press

Haunted Telford

PHILIP SOLOMON

From heart-stopping accounts of apparitions and manifestations, to first-hand encounters with spirits, this collection of stories contains both new and well-known spooky stories from in and around Telford. It is sure to fascinate everyone with an interest in the area's history.

978 0 7524 5766 6

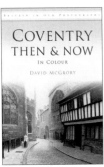

Coventry Then & Now

DAVID MCGRORY

The historic city of Coventry has a rich heritage, which is uniquely reflected in this fascinating compilation. Contrasting a selection of eighty archive images alongside full-colour modern photographs, this book captures how the city used to be and how it looks today. As well as delighting the many tourists who visit the city, *Coventry Then & Now* will provide present occupants with a glimpse of how the city used to be, in addition to awakening nostalgic memories for those who used to live or work here.

978 0 7524 5994 3

Hanged at Birmingham

STEVE FIELDING

For decades the high walls of Birmingham's Winson Green Gaol have contained some of the country's most infamous criminals. Steve Fielding's highly readable new book features each of the forty cases in one volume for the first time and is fully illustrated with rare photographs, documents, news cuttings and engravings. *Hanged at Birmingham* will appeal to everyone interested in the darker side of the region's history.

978 0 7524 5260 9

The Story of Brewing in Burton on Trent

ROGER PROTZ

Beer has been made in the small Midland town of Burton on Trent for centuries: ale brewed by the monks at Burton Abbey was sent to Mary, Queen of Scots in captivity. Raise a glass to Burton's unique and heady history, and celebrate its diverse and delicious heritage with this fascinating and richly illustrated historical compilation by *The Good Beer Guide's* editor, Roger Protz.

978 0 7524 6063 5

Visit our website and discover thousands of other History Press books.

www.thehistorypress.co.uk